The Sin Which Doth Easily Beset Us

My Personal Autobiography

Michael C. Wright

KJV
Scripture quotations marked KJV are from the Holy Bible, King James Version (Authorized Version). First published in 1611. Quoted from the KJV Classic Reference Bible, Copyright © 1983 by The Zondervan Corporation.

Printed in the United States of America.

Library of Congress Control Number: 2016905877

| ISBN | Paperback | 978-1-68536-327-7 |
| | eBook | 978-1-68536-328-4 |

Westwood Books Publishing LLC
Atlanta Financial Center
3343 Peachtree Rd NE Ste 145-725
Atlanta, GA 30326

www.westwoodbookspublishing.com

The Sin Which Doth So Easily Beset Us
By: Michael C. Wright—Ordained Chaplain

Hebrews 12:1

"Wherefore seeing we also are compassed about with so great a cloud of witnesses, let us lay aside every weight, and *the sin which doth so easily beset us,* and let us ___run with patience___ the race that is set before us."

Contents

Prologue, by Reverend Moisés Garo, Pastor, IDDPMI, Carol City, FL.

The author, characterized by his enthusiasm, his wide and spontaneous smile, his loquacity and ease with which he makes friends, is a native born Afro-American who is fluent in a few foreign languages. At first glance one might think him to be a dark-skinned, intrepid Latin of who when speaking, displays shades of American expression. He is a natural leader refined by his military experience. He is a chaplain who serves with gusto in his ministry. In this small book, he completely bares his soul, uncovering areas where many would never reveal until they were dead and to be sure, none of us would have ever suspected he was susceptible to unless we happened to read his book.

In his preadolescent years, he regrettably had to endure the dysfunction of divorce in his parent's marriage. He and his siblings had to be removed from their home and live with an uncle in Birmingham, Alabama, while his mother was reestablished in Cleveland, Ohio. The children were told what was happening thusly: "This is all for the best", and "This is only going to be for a little while." They were also told: "Don't worry. You'll be alright." But the separation was definitive. The marriage was over. "As you can imagine—he remarked—this news was devastating to the children."

After some time, his mother was diagnosed with the disease of Lupus, from which she would eventually succumb to and die. "That news pretty much destroyed everybody. Even daddy, who I had never seen cry before, did so on that day", he affirms. "The funeral service was extremely sad." He notes how the adults received words of comfort and encouragement, but not even one word of similar consolation was offered to the children by the adult attendees.

Perhaps, the absence of his parents in those critical years explains in part, the experiences he shares in this book. There were some beautiful moments that he enjoyed alongside his father, because he was able to work with him during the summer month vacations from school and his father paid him $90.00. He comments: "I thought that was quite a bit back then. Daddy said I should use it for the up-and-coming school year. It was not so bad an experience though. During one of those vacation months, he and his father went fishing and his father saw a water moccasin crossing the lake. The moccasin "…swam into the banks to the left of us about 20 yards or so, and slithered up and out of sight….I must admit"—says the author, "…I felt pretty safe with my father at that time and wished in my own way that we could have more moments like that." The book, as was said earlier, is a step into the author's interior. Transparently and simply, he explains the reason which moved him to write it: "…soul confession to the body of Christ is another step towards spiritual and ministerial transparency and healing…" With that sentence, the doors which guard the rooms of his heart are flung open in order to show just how much he prostrated and yielded himself to lust from the time of his youth. It is unusual to ask forgiveness from all who read, but he in retrospect, understands that he in some way, has failed all who read.

He deeply loves and admires his wife. He expresses it many times and in many way throughout the book. Here is some of what he says: "She is woman of the highest virtue and without her, I am absolutely sure I would not be who I am today." "Lucy, my beloved…I love you so much…it is you that has been a blessing in my life…I do not deserve you…I thank God that He has put you in my way. I will always love you." Regarding his encounter with her in Europe, while she travelled from Holland to Bettembourg, in Luxembourg, he seemed lost in placid and secret thought contemplating the arrival of his beloved wife, when he said: "Boy, was I ever glad to see her there! She looked beautiful…We chatted all the way from the airport to our apartment…"

His wife, Lucy Wright, is a much loved pastor by all of us. A leader of temperance and maturity. A true woman of God who irradiates love and simplicity. A person of faith, ability and full of tenderness and peace, humble and patient. For a long time she tolerated her husband's failures, because she believed that the All-Powerful could free him from the sin that beset him. And so it was.

His conversion, as were many other happenings in the author's life, was something marvelous and unusual. He gave his life to the Lord, without anyone preaching to him. In many ways, the Creator gave him visions and transcendent experiences which in turn, made him understand the emptiness and worthlessness of his life; likewise, what his eternal destination would end up being was made clear, without the glory of God. A vivid picture of hedonism, confusion and superficiality of the author is painted during those times, which provoked him to search diligently for what he lacked in those areas, until that search led him to the only Begotten Son, Jesus Christ, who made sense out of human existence.

He had his first steps in the faith among a catholic, charismatic group, where he also received the baptism in the Holy Spirit and fire. The Lord Jesus Christ promised that the Holy Spirit would lead all those who desire to do the will of God. This was effectively fulfilled in him. One day, God showed him a picture of his life, as it were, void of sense and of values. He was given a vision of hell. The Holy Spirit moved him to come out of the Catholic Church. He was led to read the entire Bible through many times. Brothers and ministers were put in his way so as to facilitate his spiritual growth.

This work, although a bit extensive, is very intense. It could be useful in order to understand how horrible the effects of absent parents can be on children. It helps to understand how strong the ties of sin are and the difficulty one goes through when trying to escape the slavery of pornography and its' malevolent companions: Onanism (masturbation), degradation of the nature and sanctity of sex, consciousness of sin, illicit sex, wantonness, lies, hypocrisy, disrespect, and inconsideration of one's married partner, among other things.

Here is revealed the everlasting fight of a man desirous to be honest before God, before his conscience and before those that surround him.

Here is manifested his constant pain, bitterness, anxiousness and even his desperate cry before each failing and after each rising. Something that came to be of a cyclical nature and humbling routine in his life. A putrefied ulcer of sorts, difficult to heal or to feign.

He outlines in the book, effective guidelines for freedom from this slavery that affects millions of people, some of whom are Christians, according to data and statistics. His experience as a military leader, as a minister of the Lord and as a professional psychotherapist and above all, as someone who has come out of that dark captivity, are sufficient credentials in order to help those who still remain prostrate on the ground of pornographic addiction, masturbation, illicit sex or any other pernicious habit that still enslaves them.

Moreover, the book is a trip through various countries and cultures which puts on display the strong life experiences of the author on three different continents.

Read this book. It is, in the words of the author, "a step towards spiritual and ministerial transparency and healing" which will allow the reader a glimpse inside the dark labyrinths of the sin which beset him. It is evidence that God frees from sin all those who are determined to seek his help.

Pastor Moisés Garó
December 2015

Collaboration by Reverend Alejandro Aponte, Pastor, IdDPMI, Lake Worth II, FL

May God bless Ordained Chaplain Michael Wright and his beloved wife, Reverend Lucy Wright and all her family. Throughout this book, we shall witness his impactful testimony of how he was able to overcome and attain God's purpose in his life. May he encounter success in all that he purposes to achieve in his life.

Reverend
Alejandro Aponte

Dedication

If anyone deserves to be recognized and honored, first it would undoubtedly be my God and Savior, Jesus Christ, who despite my many faults and innumerable failings, has seen fit to have mercy upon my life and retain me in the ministry. I do not deserve such unfathomable love. Truly, after understanding how vile and how unworthy of his mercy I am, He nevertheless looked beyond my human inconsistencies and saw something redeemable in me, although I do not know what? May his name be glorified forever.

After my holy God Yahweh and my Savior Jesus Christ, second in line of those worthy of recognition is my beloved wife of my youth, who for 34 years, has had patience with this servant. When she found out about my human faults and how since my youth, I have been struggling with this demon in me, she did not opt to leave, nor did she ask for a divorce, though she had every right to. To the contrary, she worked hand-in-hand with me, forgiving my lies, deceptions and dishonesty and with justified anger and indignation until I was able to finally overcome this affliction that I had allowed to dominate me for so long. She is woman of the highest virtue and without her, I am absolutely sure I would not be who I am today. I will never leave her and as we stated in our marriage vows: "...until death do us part..." Thank God she took them seriously. "Lucy, my beloved...I love you so much...it is you that has been a blessing in my life...I do not deserve you...I thank God that He has put you in my way. I will always love you."

Thirdly, few are the ministers who occupying lofty positions, have the time to listen to ministers of less importance. Nonetheless there was one presbyter in particular whose name shall remain anonymous, who acted contrary to this stereotype. When I approached him to pour out my agony and heartache over this corrupt vice, he was not repulsed with me (though he also had every right to be so) but rather he prayed with this heartsick servant, crying with him at the altar in his church. Later, I accepted the discipline meted out to me because it was for the good of my soul. So, to the reader who decides to read the story of this repentant and humbled servant, I ask forgiveness also of you for having been negligent when I should have been more vigilant. But know also that even as the psalmist David declares in his famous Psalm 51:3 KJV "I acknowledge my transgressions; and my sin *is* ever before me", so I have also felt that this is when God has loved me the most and he never abandoned me. I can say with all certainty that He has restored the joy of my salvation and has allowed me to continue winning souls for his glory and honor. I believe that this is one of the most painful things I have ever had to do in my life, but if soul confession to the body of Christ is another step towards spiritual and ministerial transparency and healing, (no one has obligated me to do this, but I have felt the Holy Spirit move me to share this testimony) then with pleasure I shall do it.

May God bless all those ministers, pastors, brothers and sisters in the faith that have prayed for and with me. I do not deserve your friendship but I know that a true friend, be it man or woman, is not only present when things are good, but also when they are bad. To this end they stay, until such time as he who is overtaken in a fault be restored and renewed by the love, mercy and grace of our God. I am that person. I extend heartfelt thanks to "Pure Life Ministries", based in Kentucky, which offered me opportune counsel and attacked the root of my addiction, which in turn was extremely beneficial in helping in the recuperation of my integrity, spirituality and the final breaking of that cursed addiction. May God bless the men and women who work there, who are more empathetic, having walked that path themselves in another time. Worthy of equal mention is the little book: Sexual Temptation by the Christian author Randy Alcorn. Short and brief, but nonetheless powerful in its message to those who are trapped in this vice and addiction. All these means really helped me in my fight against the sin which so easily beset me. May God also bless Brother Randy.

I would like to share that in my most recent profession as a psychotherapist in the addiction field, I see the irony of one being able to help others with the problems and at the same time, not being able to help oneself. This is something quite counterproductive, which certainly is destined to fail sooner or later. So what follows, despite the fact that it is a personal testimony, is likewise a testimony of what God does with his children in order to better them until such time as his light shines brilliantly in them. It speaks of how God let me go through so many trails of fire so that in the end they would make me more emphatic, sensible and compassionate towards all those who might have addictions, whatever they may be. Before, I could not understand why a person could not control himself, if he were taken by surprise with some fault, sin, weakness or mania. It's not that I thought myself better than them, but I simply couldn't see why they could not control such addictions by sheer human will. Now, I see clearly that we are all at different stages of progress in our daily walk with our Lord and Savior Jesus Christ. If Jesus has the patience to wait until we are all perfected in him, who do I think I am not to want the same for all my brothers and sisters in the universal church of Jesus Christ?

The bible says in Galatians 6:1 (KJV) "Brethren, if a man be overtaken in a fault, ye which are spiritual, restore such an one in the spirit of meekness, considering thyself, lest thou also be tempted." And for many years I indeed was tempted and failed because of my own concupiscence. But now I can say: "Thank you God, for this revelation so great and yet so simple that you have shown me in my life. I love you with all my heart and I will serve you the rest of my life until I die, because you allowed me to see now what I could not for many years. A thousand thanks and amen to my blessed Lord and Savior Jesus Christ.

Chapter 1

To an athletic person, this inspirational verse Hebrews 12:1 (KJV) makes sense, because when an athlete knows he or she is to participate in an event requiring endurance, they may be inclined to use ankle, shoulder or leg weights to build up their strength. When they shed those weights, they seem to be exhilarated by the feelings of momentary lightness they experience. Having shed those weights, they can now they can now jump higher, run faster and endure longer distances. If the author of the book of Hebrews knew this, then it's just a matter of logical deduction that we who love the word of God should also try and heed his advice. If there is a paradox to this exhortation, it would be that we should undertake the race that awaits us with patience. The very idea of running a race implies velocity and taking advantage of one's own speed. Most athletes want to finish the race as quickly as possible and depending on the event they have chosen to compete in, that usually makes sense. The athlete that finishes *first*, wins the prize. Simple, is it not? Nevertheless, when it comes to the 'Christian race', most of us don't know what kind of "event" we might face from day to day. It is hard to plan a strategy if we don't know what we're up against, one could say. That is why Jesus gave us his words of wisdom when he said: "Take therefore no thought for tomorrow: for the morrow shall take thought for the things of itself. Sufficient unto the day is the evil thereof." Matt 6:34 KJV In this race we're set to run, we do not know from one day to the next, what the event might be that we have to run through or to, as the case might be. That is why we need to *have patience to run* the 'Christian race.' This is the point where I imagine the reader might ask: "And what does this have to do with you?" So very glad you asked that question. Actually, much and in many ways, because it describes my struggle almost to a tee. Admittedly, I am starting my story "pre-Christ" and not "post Christ".

My beloved mother when she was younger. Isn't she beautiful?

My Dad when he was younger. My mother told
us she found him to be handsome.

I must also confess that it is not without the deepest shame that I share portions of my personal testimony here, but to do any less would be a disservice to the concept of transparency and *sustained*, consistent integrity, two virtues which I highly cherish but which also have eluded me for decades. If I expect others to be that way, I certainly must be willing to be the first to display as much. So, here is my "beginning", or at least, what I consider to be a satisfactory beginning for the reader. To be sure, it is not complete because to do so, would be to include two volumes or more but what follows can be classified as a brief autobiography. My purpose is simply to confess my faults and also to warn anyone who might be contemplating doing the same to seriously think about it at least **five** times and if after doing so, they still wish to entertain the idea of becoming enmeshed in such vices, (God forbid) then be prepared to be thrusted through with an innumerable amount of pain, sadness and almost unbearable sorrow. Now you know. 1 John 1:9-10 (KJV) continues to be true in the lives of those that believe God and his word. It declares: "If we confess our sins, he is faithful and just to cleanse us all unrighteousness. If we say we have sinned not, we make him to be a liar and his word dwelleth not in us." Amen and amen. Allow me to direct the reader's attention to Webster's dictionary and how it defines the following word: *Beset: transitive verb. 1. To set or stud with or as if with ornaments. 2. Trouble, harass<inflation besets economy> 3a. To set upon: assail.* (Italics mine) www.merriam-webster.com The definitions which best describes me would be numbers 2 and 3. Why? Because simply put, ***I have allowed lust, lasciviousness and concupiscence to cause me trouble*** from a very early age, although it was not openly evident to anyone at the time. No one twisted my hand, held a gun to my head or forced me to embrace it. It was an unfortunate path I chose. Nevertheless when I ignorantly opened the door to it, there was no end to the internal anxiety I experienced. This is **the sin** which throughout my natural, spiritual and ministerial life has so easily beset me. Likewise, it assailed my senses, assaulted my morals, and shipwrecked what should have been decent thoughts and acceptable moral conduct throughout adolescence. Hundreds of thousands of other adolescents my

A family photo with grandma (passed away) when she was 98 years old. She lived to be 103 years old. SSG Wright was overseas when this photo was taken. From right to left (standing first row up) Davette, Dana, Lois, and Lori. (Bottom row) Stephanie, GR ANDMA, Tommy and my nephew, David.

age did **not** choose to do this. I don't mean to give the impression that I was a raging pervert. Quite the contrary, anyone who knew me, even then would say I was well-mannered, obedient, and respectful young man to my elders and rarely caused any major trouble. I just gave into my youthful lust at the time, and "tried it", if you will.

"It", could be aptly described as the 'gateway' to other sins (just as it is widely supposed that marijuana is a gateway drug to other drugs which later on become highly addictive) which affected me as well, later on in life. And what exactly was "It"? It was masturbation—which later on in my final teen years peaked my curiosity about pornography—which of course, as you might expect, took away my inhibitions regarding illicit sex. The rest, as they say, is history. In reality, it is **MY** story but I will admit, to this day, it still remains a mystery to me as to why I allowed all of this *misery,* pain and corruption to influence me as it did.

Carnal thoughts, words, deeds or action never crossed my mind when I was a child of 9 or 10. Even as I entered into puberty at 11 or 12, I still had no real clue what the "birds and the bees" or what sexual concepts were about. In a family of five girls and two boys, that was no easy feat, but my parents were just that loving, strict and careful so as to ensure that carnal knowledge would not affect their children until such time as they saw fit. Sure, almost every child hears sexual innuendos from unlearned, unqualified and sometimes ignorant sources, like their older brothers, best friends or even their enemies in a fight or something of this nature. Speaking for myself at least, I heard expressions which I knew would never have been done, even in my wildest, sickest dreams. Those are the ages in which many children are protected from salacious influences because of the familial cocoon that surrounds and protects them. Responsible parents generally try extremely hard to protect their little ones from learning about these realities too early. This of course, is exactly how it should be in the writer's estimation, because a child should have time to be a child and experience childish things, as it were. If God's natural and wholesome plan is followed, there will be enough time for learning about life for adolescent children and generally speaking, that knowledge should be imparted to them by their parents, exceptions notwithstanding. In the same vein, most parents know that this ideology does not always work. Given the imperfect world we live in, for some innocent children, it's just a matter of time before they will be affected positively or negatively by sexual influences sooner or later. Parents then, logically try and make it a positive experience if and when that time arrives.

My father and mother began having marital problems when we were all fairly young and by the time I was around eleven years old or so, we were told (my younger brother and younger, middle and eldest sister) that we would be going to live in Birmingham, Alabama with an uncle.

As you might imagine, this was devastating news to us kids, who really, *really* didn't want to leave "mommy", as we always affectionately called her. But, at that age, what choice or say so did we have? "It's for the best; it's only be for a little while," we were told. "But when will we see you again?" we asked. "Don't worry. You all will be alright." Or something to that affect is what I recall if my memory serves me correctly. So, that's what we did. Years later we found out that mommy was sick with Lupus, which wasn't easily diagnosed back in the mid-sixties. After several misdiagnoses, she eventually was taken to a Jewish doctor in Cleveland, Ohio who specialized in determining this rare type of cancer and after about 3 years, we were sent to stay with a dear aunt and uncle while she tried to recover from it.

Seeing mommy again was one of the greatest moments to me, and was quite emotional. She hugged and kissed us and we cried a lot. Later, when our grandmother (who also lived in Shaker Heights, Ohio), told us that mommy was not doing well and she might not live that much longer, it shook us to the core. Visiting her in the hospital brought back memories to me of when she (and Daddy, at the time before they separated and eventually divorced) visited me in the hospital when we were still living in Massachusetts. I came down with spinal meningitis and almost died from it, but after a 2-week stay there, they contained it and I went home with my parents. Now, here we were seeing her, which made us all the sadder. We didn't really understand everything that was going on but to be quite honest, I didn't care about any of that. I just

15

wanted mommy to get well, but I was powerless to stop whatever it was that was making her sick. Heartbreakingly, she succumbed to Lupus and it devastated everyone—even my dad, who I had never seen cry, but that day he did cry. The funeral was a sad affair and though there were many people there offering condolences, I can't recall any of my siblings nor I being consoled at that time or many years later. My grandmother was quite bitter because she felt that if daddy hadn't brought so much trauma and pain on her *only* daughter, she might not have ended up this way. My cousins, older and middle sister and my younger brother were witness to all of this and it affected all in different ways. A year or so after this, at around age 14, somewhere and somehow, in my moments of curiosity, inquisitiveness and frustration is when I learned about masturbation and tried it for the first time.

It both scared me to death, appalled me that I would do that (having been exposed to catholic teachings up to that point, which most certainly did not condone such conduct, nor most others, as far as I know) and at the same time, exhilarated me. I did not do it again until years later until we moved once again to Massachusetts but I did inadvertently open the door to carnal influences which would eventually affect me for years to come. That is why I hid when doing these things because of the shame I would experience should someone ever find out. My older cousin told me (in Ohio) that he knew I had done this but he didn't think it was such a big deal. Matter of fact, he laughed at it. That relieved me a little bit, but the shame never went away, because I knew in my heart that I shouldn't be doing this, otherwise, why would I hide when doing it?

Daddy eventually found employment in the furniture transportation field as a trucker or "18-Wheeler", as these men and women were popularly called back then. He announced one summer that he would be coming to take me (his eldest) with him. Because my younger brother was not quite old enough to use as a helper on the truck, I suppose he decided against taking him with us on that one occasion. Truth be told, I was kind of excited that I'd be getting away from Cleveland and going with him, although I didn't quite know how I'd feel towards him since Mommy had passed away and all. In any case, there was really nothing I could do about it. So, summer came and sure enough, Daddy showed up in the big old rig that had 'Mayflower' written all over it. I thought: "Why do they have a picture of a ship painted on the side of a truck?" not having a clue that the picture referred to a time when America was in its' early stages and ships were the most popular mode of transportation over the oceans and seas in that time period. I learned that and much more information that my father shared with me during our trip together. I can't recall as I ever worked as hard. Daddy said I was something he called "free labor" because I was his son and he didn't have to pay me. (I think they might call this concept child abuse nowadays).

"See them clothes you got on?", he asked. "Yes sir", I answered. "I send money every month to your aunt for you, your brother and sister so that she can buy you what y'all need, understand?" "Un huh", I answered, even though I didn't but, I was scared to say so. Daddy could be intimidating when he wanted to, especially when he was alone with you. He didn't do it to be mean, but he was "driven" so to speak, to prove something, or so it seemed. (Perhaps to prove to my grandmother that he could indeed take care of all his children, even in the face of my mother's passing away. It appeared as though she told him as much, so maybe he *was* trying to prove that he could, through hard work and a job which paid him enough to take care of us all). To be fair though, he did give me about $90 dollars, although it's hard to remember if it was every month or for the whole three months we were on the road. I thought that was quite a bit back then. He said I should use it for the up and coming school year. It was not so bad an experience though. We even went fishing. That was when daddy saw a big water moccasin crossing the lake with the greatest of ease. He pointed it out to me saying: "Look, look, Michael!" It swam into the banks to the left of us about 20 yards or so and slithered up and out of sight. I must admit I felt pretty safe with my father at that time and wished in my own way that we could have more moments like that. In my own little mind, I knew it was a good thing to be together as a family. That's why it was hard to understand why it couldn't be like this all the time.

As we continued in our travels, I was also introduced to something I now know was not good for a young man to find out about either. That was racism. Neither my father nor I expected it to happen as it did. While making a delivery in Meridian Mississippi, I guess some men down there didn't like the color of our skin and while we were sleeping, one of them went under the cab and cut the brake lines, knowing that in the morning, we would be headed for a very steep incline. They knew we wouldn't be able to recover from that and would have been killed. Thank God, my father realized it before he actually hit the incline because out of habit, he always did his morning maintenance check of his rig. That's when I learned that you couldn't trust all white men and daddy didn't trust *any* of them, or so it seemed to me at the time.

Unfortunately, that was also where (and I don't know why), let my lusts get a hold of me and masturbated once during that summer. Daddy slept in the cab and he told me to sleep in the back trailer where there were plenty of pads that we used to cover furniture and other items. This was more towards the end of the trip and so much at the beginning, but regardless of when it was, I unwittingly opened a door that would take decades to shut completely. Hindsight, as they say, is always 20/20 but it is true that had I known this sin would be so pernicious; I would have never entertained it. That statement does not really mean much because just about everyone who's been caught in a forbidden or shameful act or sin say that. Just the same, I cannot emphasize enough times how repentant and remorseful I was over the fact that I allowed this to affect me for decades on end. May I briefly interject in parenthesis, as it were, by saying here that I have been blessed to work in a variety of employs over the years. Nevertheless, when I obtained a master's degree in social work with a specialty track in drug/alcohol counseling, (and I've worked with other populations as well) it allowed me to have a unique perspective on those caught up in addictions, no matter what they might be. One could observe both the practical and spiritual side. Why is that important? Because I also had an addiction. It is not difficult for me to empathize and identify with them because as the saying goes: "It takes one to know one." Although the addiction may be different, the pattern of deceit, manipulation, exasperation and desperation often appear to be the same. Nevertheless, there is no feeling like the one received when a broken heart has been mended, a child has had his or her smile restored, or therapy has helped restore your client's healthy outlook on life. This is the feeling when the addict has obtained sustained sobriety or autonomy over the vice or addiction that held them in bondage for some many years. Depending on one's specialty within the social work field, it is highly unlikely that one will *not* come across broken or dysfunctional families who need counseling. More often than not, those family units contain hurting, dysfunctional parents who in turn raise or abuse their children. Of course the child is not at fault for the abuse that occurs. Returning now to my story. Again, Hebrew 12:1 states: "…the sin with doth easily beset us…" My struggles with overcoming pornography could not be summed up any better. Returning home to Cleveland and enrolling in middle school was normal. Nothing happened from the age of around 14 through 17. Student peer interaction was regular and what you would expect from boys that age. The school at that time was Cleveland Central Catholic and that is where I continued to develop an attraction to music which my father had sparked in my siblings and I when we were just kids of 10 or less. My beautiful aunt, stern uncle and rambunctious cousins left an indelible impression on me which for the most part was always positive. After all, we were living with them and they were doing a favor for my dad by taking us in. With the passage of time, my dad eventually remarried, bought a big 13-room house in Massachusetts and sent for his children to reunite us all. It was not easy for any of us to adapt to his new wife, although she was not a bad person. It's just that in the mind of most children and adolescents, nobody can take the place of your natural mother. By this time, we were enrolled in high school and my academic performance could be categorized as average. By the time graduation came, I had actually gone to two high schools but the last two years were spent at Commerce High School. A point of curiosity, my name was "David Michael Wright" throughout my beginning school years until my high school graduation. This was because of a rift between my mother and father over him wanting a son named after him and what was actually on the birth certificate. Confused? So was I.

Prom night? Never went because I did not have a girlfriend and I didn't it see as being so important. But in truth, I was a little sad inside. On the other hand, I did have a good friend nicknamed "Butchy" and he and I were practically inseparable during those years.

Daddy taught me the normal things teenage boys should know, like repairing my '67 Chevy and not drinking too much liquor, but never really talked that much about sexual themes, so what I picked up came from a variety of unreliable sources, exaggerated schoolyard stories and elder sister admonishments. My elder sisters by this time were out and on their own and had their husband or boyfriends with whom they were living. My relationship with my father was becoming somewhat strained and there was one particular time I recall when he wanted me help him do something with a car he was repairing and I just didn't want to because Butchy and me wanted to go out. He yelled my name all around the house but couldn't find me because I was hiding in the garage, (kind of on purpose). When I finally showed myself, he was fit to be tied and I said something smart to him and he punched me and knocked me on the ground. I didn't dare get up and through clenched fists and threatening speech he basically said that if I ever did that again he would knock me into the middle of next week, and I'm here to tell you, he would have done it too. That incident was a wakeup call for me. The summer of my graduation, I asked my father if he could send me to college because I had seen my older sisters attend college with his approval. He said he couldn't because he didn't have the money but suggested that if I wanted to go, a good way would be through the military. Since our relationship was becoming noticeably more strained, I thought that might be a good idea. Ironically, Butchy wasn't getting along too well with his parents either and when I shared what my father had suggested, he said his 'old man' had told him pretty much the same thing.

So, as teenage boys will do, we made a pact that day to go into the military (Air Force) through their delayed entry program. That would give us enough time to tie up any loose ends and the Air Force agreed and we could go in under the "Buddy" program. As you can imagine, my father applauded the idea and he said it would make more of a man out of me. In hindsight, he was right but who knew at the time?

Believe it or not, when it came time to actually go, Butchy chickened out on me and I found myself in San Antonio, Texas going through Boot Camp alone. The screaming drill sergeants yelling at you and calling you names you never heard of brought you back to reality real quick, so there wasn't much time to be melancholy. New friendships were forged and new adventures awaited. More noteworthy still, was the fact that I could now do what parental constraint would never allow me to do. I am quite sure that the majority of young adults feel this way. The problem is we have no earthly idea of what really awaits us and at times, mistakenly think that we will do better than our parents who forged the way for us. Immaturity and ungratefulness are oftimes the reasons behind such attitudes, but reality has a way of waking up those who harbor such ideas. To be sure, I was not planning any deviate, evil thing now that I was out of sight and mind of my father, but just enjoy the freedom of adulthood. I was proud of some of the things I had been able to accomplish while in High School, such as holding a steady job and still maintaining good grades. Paying for my own piano lessons and learning how to correctly read music, even though I found out later on that one has to practice constantly to develop that skill. Nevertheless, my job at Spalding Sports manufacturing company in Chicopee, MA made me see that being a line worker for the next 20 or 30 years (as were most of the immigrants from Poland, Jamaica, Portugal and other countries were) just wasn't my 'cup of tea', as the British say. The monotony would have driven me crazy and I probably would have wound up quitting anyway. So, maybe it was for the best that things were developing as there were. One of the first things I did when I received my permanent duty station and realized I had a decent paycheck and steady income was to buy a brand new car. "Was this not a sure sign of growing independence?"

Airman Basic Wright graduating from Air Force basic in 1973.
(3rd row up, eighth aviator from the left to right.)

I thought? I participated in karate classes, learned to drink and heard more cursing than I had ever heard in my life. Strange as it may sound though, I never liked cursing or using God's name in vain. I suppose maybe some of the religious training I received as a youngster stuck. Not that I was a saint (just an altar boy for a while—and that doesn't qualify) but I always had a healthy respect for the Supreme Being, even though I did not really know who He was at the time. Unfortunately here, this is the time period in my life where the door to licentiousness, lascivious thoughts and illicit relations opened even wider. All my buddies were with girls and talking about their exploits and I didn't want to be the odd man out, if you know what I mean. Therefore, illicit sex, pornography, peep shows and all those kinds of shameful activities and opportunities availed themselves to young men whose libidos were out of control.

The most powerful preacher I have ever known in my life (and still is to this day) was my conscience. For as much as I tried to make myself look big, tough, and 'in the know', my conscience was never fooled and told me as much many times. It was just that I tried to ignore it and because I managed to do so, wound up feeling so empty at the end of various illicit sexual relationships, that I wound up attempting suicide by swallowing a bottleful of aspirins, turning out the lights in my room in the barracks (Albuquerque, New Mexico) and waiting for the end to come. All this before my 21st birthday, mind you. I cannot tell you to this day why I did not suffer the effects of having to have my stomach pumped to being rushed to the hospital because I truly did not expect to wake up the next day. But since none of those things happened, my perspective or outlook on life changed and I thought: "Well, since suicide didn't work, maybe there is a reason I'm supposed to be here, so look out world, here I come."

Not long after this, I received orders to go to paradise; not the heavenly one but the one where if you're not saved, will probably be as close as you'll get, Hawaii. As the smell of pineapples hit me when off-boarding the plane, I could not believe how lucky I was to have landed in a place like this. Beautiful girls were waiting to put a Leigh around our necks as we came off the ramp of the plane. "Wow", I thought. I never dreamed in a million years that I would ever see any place outside Massachusetts. But thinking about it, I had already lived in Alabama, then Cleveland, and later traveled to just about every state with my father as a youngster and now I was back in Massachusetts where I graduated from high school and went into military service. Now with my arrival in Oahu, Hawaii, it seemed like I was being geared up to become a world traveler. Little did I know that God was preparing me for the greatest trip of my life which and ironically enough, was also the shortest. It was only about twelve inches.

I still carried my AFSC (Air Force Specialty Code) as a security police when I arrived in Hawaii, but that was to change to a different one later on, to that of a truck driver and vehicle dispatcher. I felt quite comfortable settling into my routine while stationed at Hickam Air Force Base, Hawaii. One of the highlights of my experiences was as a flight-line security police which I feel I must interject at this point. I affirm that with these eyes, I saw a U-2 (spy plane) pilot abort an early morning attempt at take-off. To this day, I cannot tell you what exactly happened but never in my life had I seen or heard so many wailing police and emergency vehicles come out of nowhere. The pilot jumped out of the cockpit and ran to the side of the runway. Technical personnel were on the scene in what seemed to me was less than a minute. There was obviously some type of problem. After about an hour or so, it appeared as though the problem was fixed and the pilot began his take-off roll again and after using very little of the runway, literally ascended up and up into the beautiful Hawaiian clouds until he disappeared from my view. "Wow"! I thought. Was I ever glad I was there to witness that event. "Aw shucks", I thought. "Who's gonna believe me if I tell them?" "No one", I thought again. But it really did happen, so I'm satisfied in knowing that it did occur and God is my witness. Returning to my story, as time marched on, it wasn't long before more of those aforementioned opportunities raised their "attractive" heads in the form of beautiful Hawaiian and Asian girls and it doesn't require much of an imagination to figure out what went on afterwards. In one of these instances, my Hawaiian girlfriend "neglected" to tell me that she had another boyfriend on the side. So, the next morning, imagine my surprise (and his too) to see him walk in the apartment. After a heated argument between the two in the adjoining room, I was told that I should leave. Resentful that it should be me that had to leave, I went over to where my jacket was (he was partially sitting on it but didn't know it) snatched it from out under him, glaring at him as only men (or fools) do to each other. He did the same to me but the walk from the couch to the door was the longest I've ever taken in my life, especially since I perceived that he had a pistol under his shirt. Funny how we don't pray until we get into situations that obligate us to do so, but I silently prayed: "Lord, if you get me out of this mess, I will never do something like this again." He did, and I stayed true to my prayer—until I met another girl on post, pointed out to me by one of the secretaries that worked in the same office as I did. This time, the results were more pleasant, but the same feelings of emptiness abounded and a foreboding sense that what I was doing was leading me down a wrong path and if I continued therein, I might lose my life, and worse yet, my soul. Ominous thoughts for a 20- year old to have.

One enthralling Hawaiian night, as I made my way from this girl's Barracks (where I should not have been to begin with) to my shift, (3rd shift from 11pm to 7am) something strange began to happen before my eyes. There appeared above me this white, fluffy cloud that seemed to be following me, if such a thing were possible. It began to shape itself into my facial features, including my forehead, nose, eyes, chin and even the little afro that I had at the time. Tears began to sting my eyes as I said out loud: "That's me! That's me!, over and over again, as I slowly made my way to the flight line where my shift would take place. The cloud must have stayed in the sky for at least 10 minutes or so and then slowly began to dissipate. Very emotional and wondering what all of this meant, a pick-up truck full of my fellow airmen just happened to pull along side of me and the driver offered me a ride to the barracks so that I could change my clothes and be on time for my shift. I accepted but when I got in the front seat, they all seemed to notice that I had been crying or at least emotional.

"What's wrong with you man?" "Nothing", I lied." But they knew something was different about me, though they didn't pursue with their questions. I was restless all through my night shift and when it finally ended, I went to my room and wondered all day what that was about. This nagging feeling now would not leave me and something internally began to change. How did I know? For no apparent good reason I began to wait until midnight, looked to the left and to the right like a thief that's careful when he's about to steal something, then I would sneak quietly outside my dorm room and to the corner of the building where there was a big trash can. I lifted it up and threw all of my Playboy, Hustler and every other dirty magazine you could think of in the bottom of the trash can, making sure that no one else (except maybe the garbage collector) would ever see them again, because I removed all the other garbage so that the magazines would be on the very bottom. I gathered up all my marijuana paraphernalia and did the same thing. (In the 70's, we paid a lot of money to buy those marijuana pipes, hashish, tubes and etc). And, I began to read 21 chapters of the bible every night, beginning from Genesis until Revelations and I never really even knew why I chose 21 chapters rather than 3 or 10, let's say. Now, you tell me if something wasn't happening to me, or not? Mind you, not one soul, not one preacher or evangelist had spoken a word to me about Jesus, God or anything else. I'll explain. The only thing I can remember as being a catalyst was one night preceding all these events. I went out to the track stands where we customarily ran our mile and a half physical training events periodically. It was a beautiful Hawaiian might, as most of them were anyway. After sitting for about a half an hour or so in the bleachers, (about 1pm in the morning) I looked up into the sky and asked God: "Is this all there is? Is this all there is? (Referring to life itself). Of course He didn't answer me, BUT, I suppose I can say that He heard me. How do I know? Because not too long after this prayer, all of these events I'm describing to you began to happen to me. Let me also share with you a very scary vision I had while smoking marijuana one afternoon after work. It went like this:

One day after work in the room of whoever invited us there, I had what I guess can be described as a momentary vision that truly and quite literally scared the "hell" out of me. How? Now, don't ask me if it was the type or potency of the marijuana, mixed with something else. No, I don't believe it was. At any rate, while sitting down in the chair after having taken a drag from a marijuana cigarette, I suddenly found myself literally in "hell". I saw figures as far as the eye could see in thick darkness and the only thing that illuminated them was the fire emanating out of their beings. Such screams I have never heard in my life and I pray I never will as long as I live. There were literally millions and millions of people there with no apparent way to get out of there. I began to scream: "Ahhh! Get me out of here! Get me out of here!", and just like that, I was back in the room, full of marijuana smoke. The only difference was that every, single person in that room was now looking at me incredulously, wondering what on earth was the matter with me. Literally seeing hell was what made me scream. Take it for what it's worth, but that was something I **NEVER, EVER** want to experience again. Anyway, feeling embarrassed (again), I quickly excused myself and headed straight for my room. This "vision", coupled with the aforementioned experiences certainly contributed to the idea that either I was going crazy or that "something" was happening to me.

Finally, one night after having finished the bible from Genesis to Revelations, I laid it down, agreeing in my heart that what was written therein was the truth, even though I did not understand it fully. I did not wish to disturb my roommate in the bunk bed, so I quietly made my way to the half bathroom and stood in front of the big mirror over the hand wash basin. I stretched really hard and yarned but just as I was coming out of the stretch, I lost consciousness. Now, when I first came into the half bathroom, the clock next to my bed read 3 a.m. As I was unconscious, I cannot tell you where I was taken or even what happened, other than to say that near the end of the experience, it seemed as though this gigantic hand lifted the soul portion of me, and carried it until it aligned itself with my body (which was lying prone on the floor, now if front of the bunk bed) and much like a mother cat carries around her kittens in her mouth. Then, this gigantic hand groped the nape of my neck and dropped the soul portion of me and it slowly descended until it

27

became one with my body, if you can imagine such a thing happening. I opened my eyes wide as saucers and looked up, down and every which way. To say that I was shocked was the understatement of the year, but I still had the presence of mind to not want to wake up my bunk bed partner. The clock in the room read 5:45am. I crawled to my bottom bed and there, closed my eyes. Such a feeling of dread and hopelessness came over me that I couldn't even form words to speak. I felt as though I was literally hanging over the pits of hell and that there was no hope. The only thing I began saying in my mind was: "I'm sorry. I'm sorry. I'm so sorry; forgive me." Even though I never mentioned God or Jesus, somehow I supposed that they both knew that all this remorse was directed towards them. I knew internally that it was them (God the Father; Jesus the Son). I had offended them and only they could forgive my sins and it was for all those sins committed up to that point that I was sorry for. To me, that is why the tears flowed abundantly. Soon I began to verbalize this expression, mixed with tears. For as much as I tried to keep silent, it was no longer possible and I began to sob and weep and basically cry like a big baby and out loud. I could not help myself. I knew that I awoke my partner because I heard him move and saw from the corner of my eye that he looked down at me from his top bunk bed.

After a while, I felt such a feeling of warmth cover me as I had never felt in my life. It seemed as though it went from the crown of my head to the soles of my feet. It is hard to explain but in that instance, I knew I was forgiven for all of my sins I had ever committed! It truly was, as the scriptures say in Philippians 4:7 (KJV) *"And the peace of God, which passeth all understanding, shall keep hearts and minds through Christ Jesus."* I surely did not understand the peace that was invading my soul, but I was sure glad to have it there. It was more precious than any known material thing and I would never give it up for anything in this world, then or now. I suddenly knew I was saved. I could not explain it, but I knew I was saved, **really** saved! This was the TRIP that God wanted me to take all these years and it wasn't so much with my earthly father, but with my heavenly one, but I was too foolish to understand that. It never costs me money or planned coordination that He hadn't

28

already thought of beforehand. The only thing it costs me was time and a heartfelt confession, which I willingly gave. Understand that I had long since stopped attending church, obviously because the sins that I was committing were not conducive to hypocritically attending church and acting as though everything was fine in my life. Surprisingly enough, most folks I talk with while I evangelizing tell me that they don't go to a priest for confession or to the preacher or minister or pastor (if they're not catholic) because they know that what they're doing is wrong. When asked: "What would happen to you if you should die suddenly? Where would you end up at?" Again, most respond that they would probably wind up in hell (not purgatory) and they say they know because their conscious convicts them. Had someone asked me that **before** this experience, I probably would have responded the same way. But after it, a divine knowledge seemed to invade me and confirm to me internally that all was forgiven. I now knew what it felt like to be convicted of sin by the Holy Spirit, and in the same breadth, be forgiven of it. If you have never asked God to forgive you of your sins through the shed blood of his son Jesus, please do it today, while there is yet time to do so. Amen.

Needless to say, my roommate was curious as to what happened to me during the night, not to mention why I had awoken him. I tried to explain as best as I knew how what took place but he wasn't very receptive to it. When I began to speak about Jesus, God, forgiveness and the like, he became angry and stormed out of the room, slamming the door behind him.

That was my first encounter with resistance to the gospel message. I did not quite know how to handle it, but I took it in stride and shrugged it off because he was a little quirky anyway, I thought.

The best way to describe the ensuing weeks, were as if I was walking on a cloud. I had not attended mass for quite a few years, even though I was an altar boy in Ohio and went through catholic grade, middle and high school until the 9th grade. Nevertheless, suddenly, I began to attend the base chapel program. There were not many in attendance, but the catholic priest who presided over the mass, saw me and noticed that I would always have a smile on my face. Whereas most people would throw in a dollar or two when the collection plate was passed around, I would throw in $25 (quite a lot for a senior airmen in the 70s era) and would quietly leave. Not that the chapel needed the money, but one day the priest caught up with me and said he noticed I always seemed to have a smile on my face and appeared in good spirits. He asked me if I would like to attend an ongoing Wednesday night charismatic gathering they were having in another location. I had no idea what he was talking about and asked him to explain what that meant. He said the best way to describe it was for me to go and see for myself. So, I did. There, I met folks who seemed to be jovial and enthusiastic about Jesus.

One elder Hawaiian lady had the most calming and sweetest voice seemed to be prominent in the group. They sang songs with a guitar. A different priest sat in the back and did not say much. I guessed he was there more to monitor the activities as opposed to participating because he appeared to be kind of incredulous. The laymen (and women) seemed to be the ones who led the meeting from start to finish. I was grateful to God for this first of a kind experience as I was learning more about walking with Jesus. As I continued to attend those charismatic meetings, the same Hawaiian lady who led the gathering asked me one night if I spoke in tongues and if not, would I like to? Thinking she meant if I spoke another language, I affirmed that I spoke pretty good Spanish. To this, most of the attendees burst out in laughter, which of course puzzled me. She tenderly explained to me that she wasn't referring to an earthly language, but a heavenly one. I told her I had no idea what that was, but that if it was of God, I certainly wanted it. With that, a line formed for all those in attendance who wished to have the same experience. When she finally got to me, she gently laid her hands on my forehead and prayed the sweetest prayer to God that I had heard in a while. All of a sudden, something literally took hold of my tongue and out of my throat, came quiet, foreign uttering which startled me so much, I quickly opened my eyes. She lovingly assured me that there was nothing to be alarmed about, but that this experience was the Holy Spirit infilling me and encouraged me to close my eyes and enjoy the experience and let God finish his work in me, which I did. I cannot remember how many in the line received the "baptism" in the Holy Spirit (as I learned later on it was often called) or if their experience was genuine or not, but I do know that mine was and until this day, I am grateful for that Christian sister being led of God to bring that wonderful experience to me. I spoke (and still speak) in an unknown tongue for the glory of God. More importantly though, it is the motivation from the Holy Spirit that drives me to try and win souls for Christ, each time an opportunity is afforded me; to be a witness in "Jerusalem, Judea and Samaria", as it were. Wherever in the world God may lead me, in other words. Some may say the experience was of the devil, referring to speaking in tongues. To that assertion I would refer the reader to the word of God and simply ask: Does the devil give glory to God and praise the name of Jesus? Are the two not diametrically opposed? How can one fountain produce sweet and bitter water at the same time, and even if it did, would not our natural reaction be to spit it out straightway? James 3:11 (KJV) If tongues, which is given by God to those who ask Him, is of the devil, have we not now attributed evil to God? Is it not extremely dangerous to blaspheme the Holy Spirit? Matthew 12:31 (KJV). Does one not risk being exposed to hell fire by attributing evil to that which God has said is good? Luke 11:13 (KJV). Does man's unbelief make the truth of God null and void? God forbid! Yea, let God be true but every man a liar…" Rom. 3:4 (KJV). How can two walk together if they do not agree? Amos 3:3 (KJV). What fellowship hath righteousness with unrighteousness? 2 Cor. 6:14 (KJV). Thus I say that the tongues which I speak glorify only God Almighty continuously and not the devil. For me, the matter is settled.

Chapter 2

As time marched on, my dissatisfaction with my primary AFSC grew and I made this known to my superiors. They told me there was no way I would be able to get out of being a security police, so I should just settle back and enjoy the ride. Many had attempted and just about all failed, unless it was an unusual circumstance. Nevertheless, I just could not shake the feeling that I should move on to something else. So, as I recall, I prayed and asked God's help in this matter. I went to the officials in charge of the specialty I desired to be in and asked if there was a need for heavy vehicle/long-haul truck drivers. Since this was something I had watched my father do for many years, I knew I could do it as well. They enthusiastically responded "Yes", we sure do. Are you interested?" Of course I told them yes and before three weeks passed, all the arrangements were made and surprisingly enough, my squadron leader was not even angry (which usually was the case because he would be losing personnel and which could not be replaced so easily). One of the first things I learned to do as a vehicle dispatcher was learn to drive everything in the motor pool. To me, at the time, that was a wonderful thing to be able to accomplish, so I did just that. Tour buses, (like our Greyhound civilian counterparts) 8-18 wheeled trucks and tractor-trailer combines, heavy equipment, fork-lifts; you name it, I drove it. Instead of 3rd shift, I was now assigned to 1st shift, which meant I had the rest of the day available to explore things afterwards. It was while I was on this shift that I met a man named Samson Ing. He noticed me and how much I was always smiling and being friendly. One of the first things he said was "Praise the Lord Brother, without even knowing who I was. So, I shook his big, hand which seemed to swallow up mine. He asked me if I would like to come along with him on a run to the flight line, so I did. We would normally pick up incoming flight personnel from C-141s, C-5s and Tankers and various other planes from off the flight line. Brother Samson (or as I called him, "Sam") shared his family history in Oahu, his Christian testimony of conversion, and where he attended church. Sam was a pretty big guy with wide shoulders that fit his 6', 2" 260lb frame, whose lineage was Chinese-Hawaiian. But he also had a contagious laugh which had a tendency to render one's natural defense mechanisms useless. Soon we found ourselves chatting, trading stories and just plain getting alone quite well. As I explained to him what had been my short time in the Lord and what I believed was my conversion story to Christianity, he invited me to attend his church and added: "If it's the Lord's will that you stay in the catholic church, you will, but if not, you'll come out from among them, be separate and be a part of our church." I did not know quite how to process what he had said, because no one had ever invited me to their church and up until that point, attending the Wednesday night meetings was all I knew.

On a subsequent occasion after one of the Wednesday gatherings was ending, I mentioned to the head of the gatherings and the priest who always seemed to monitor the meetings that someone had invited me to visit their church. I also should mention that since reading the bible, I had noticed that it had a lot to say about idolatry, worshipping images and praying to God only through Jesus, without the need for an intermediate such as Mary. All of these things were present when we went to mass and they bothered me internally, but I had no one to voice my concerns with. In the time that I had been with Sam on his flight line runs, he had explained to me much of the fallacy, errors and misinterpretation of the bible that went on within the catholic institution, although he did not limit it to just Catholicism.

So, there was doubt in my mind as to whether I was following God's perfect will by being there and participating in rituals which clearly were unbiblical and highly idolatrous. Therefore, later on in the week at the Wednesday night gathering, the only one who seemed to be irate and upset that I might be considering leaving or simply visiting another church was the priest-monitor. Later, I had asked him when we were alone why do we worship Mary, why the need for rosary beads, scapulars, confessing to even a priest like himself, who had no authority to forgive sins when he was just as sinful as everyone else? All of these questions seemed to upset him more (especially the last one) and I observed a side of him I had not known before. A side which I did not like and did not seem to be appropriate for someone who was supposed to be God's representative here on the earth.

Also, he smoked cigarettes quite a bit after each service and though that may not mean much, even as a kid I thought there was something wrong with a minister doing that. To be fair though, I also saw that in the Baptist church too, not to mention my own parents at home. So, the next Sunday, I gladly went with Brother Sam to his Assemblies of God church and knew within my spirit that this was the place God wanted me to be. I have never looked back since that time, which was about 40 years ago. In those days, I was so enamored by this new experience that as I grew to know the pastor of the church, the members of the congregation (many of whom had similar testimonies of having come out of Catholicism) and the engrossing stories of missionaries going to and returning from the missionary field.

I could only thank God for leading me down the path of righteousness. Pastor Ah You, (the pastor of the A/G church) saw my dedication to his church and after about a year, threw the keys to the church to me and simply said: "Lock the church door after you're through Mike." I was accustomed to staying after the service so long that I would be the only one left and sometimes, it would be 12:01am before I would leave. I would just sit for hours thinking how good God had been to me and what more could I do to help out the brethren and the local church. I already participated in every activity they had, including playing the piano for individuals and the church choir, ascending to the head of the men's ministry (even though I was single and the position was supposed to be headed by a married man) and evangelizing with church members through the Palisades community of Pearl City at that time and I believe still is.

If the lives of Christians are to be refined, shaped or fashioned through experiences, then I understand better now, an experience which I did not quite understand when it happened. Case in point: One night when "Sam" and I had returned from the flight line, we were having our own personal bible study and in good spirits. Sam happened to forget something in the double-wide trailer that served as an office for us and he asked me to go and get it. Prior to this, they had been people, government employees with whom I worked who were not receptive to the gospel message I would try and share with them; in fact some of them were downright hostile to it. Two of these people, (one was a Hawaiian and the other was a blond lady, married with three children) either made a mockery of the gospel message or outright blasphemed the name of God. So it was, that when I opened the door to that trailer, it was dark and I automatically flipped the light switch on and proceeded to the interior office. As I approached, I heard a frantic rustling around and much noise, which startled me because no one was supposed to be in there. Lo and behold, guess who I found almost naked and in a compromising sexual position right there on the floor of the office? Exactly! The very same two people who had blasphemed the name of the Lord and mocked the gospel! I have never seen a color of red to match that of their faces that night. Neither of the two could literally look me in the eyes. I must admit, I was shocked to, as they were the last persons in the world I would have imagined were secrets lovers who would be caught in the act of adultery that fateful night. After a few seconds, I shut off the light and left in disgust and went back and told Sam what I had just witnessed. He could hardly believe it either and questioned me at least three times to make sure I knew who and what I was talking about. After that, he just shook his head in disgust too. The scripture he emphasized to me was: "Be sure your sins shall find you out." Numbers 32:23 (KJV). They had arrogantly thought God did not exist and flippantly flaunted their noses at Him. We looked at the scripture which said: "Pride goeth before destruction and a haughty spirit before a fall". Proverbs 16:18 (KJV). I learned so many lessons that night that never would have stayed with me otherwise. Here it is, 40 years since it happened and it is still clear in my mind. The reason God allowed me to experience that was to

1. Not to imitate nor condone such conduct.
2. To pray for people who give in to such temptations.
3. To know that nothing hidden will stay that way forever, but truth, though prolonged, shall prevail eventually.
4. No one that blasphemes the name of the Lord shall go blameless.
5. God defends his servants that walk in innocence and righteousness, though how He does it is sometimes a mystery to us.

These were very good lessons for a young man who was barely starting his Christian walk to learn, don't you think? I do know that from that day on, every time I saw those two, it was extremely hard for them to look me in the eye or greet me and they avoided ever instance where they might have to be alone in the office with me. I know now that was the shame they felt and the Holy Spirit convicting them of their sinful lifestyle. I did not judge them then, nor do I today. But for the grace of God, their go I. But I did learn that it is best to leave vengeance in God's hands.

Since that time I have unfortunately seen many more such cases, even in Christian circles but I have come to understand that unless we stay connected to God and resist these temptations, none of us is exempt from falling into similar situations, God forbid. I suppose one could say, I was in my "first love" with Jesus. I also had the opportunity to see and hear traveling evangelists and see miracles and signs performed in their ministries. Brother Samson had become somewhat of a spiritual father for me, so I leaned heavily on him for advice as far as who was safe to listen to or who was not. Thus, if I went downtown or to another church or anywhere to hear someone new, you can bet that he was usually with me. My only regret was that I had not been converted earlier, even though I was only 20 years old and left there when I was

23. Even more endearing was the fact that in this one church, there were many ethnicities represented; something which I had not seen much while growing up as a youngster. It was either all Caucasians in the Catholic Church, or all Blacks in the Baptist Church, which is where Daddy would take us to when we were younger and nothing in between, at least as far as my experience went. So, if I wasn't with Brother Samson in his home, then I would be with Brother and Sister Yamamoto in their home, or at some church event where I would always see Asians, Samoans, Blacks, Hawaiians, Filipinos, Chinese, Caucasians, Portuguese, Japanese and everything in between all of those. I simply loved the variety and in my simplistic way of thinking imagined that this is probably the way God wants all churches and even the human race to act towards each other. Amen.

My, how the time went by so fast! Then, before I knew it, the end of my first hitch was winding down in Hawaii. While actively involved in the church in Pearl City, I met and made friends with a God-fearing older pastor named Rugwell. We hit it off so well that he invited me to one of the other Hawaiian Islands (there are 7 or 8 in the chain) where he was pastoring after I cleared my squadron responsibilities. Since I was not attached to anyone or anything, I accepted. In hindsight, that to me, was one of the best decisions of my life. Why? Because for the first time in my life, God was teaching me though experiences, how we must live by faith and trust in Him for all provisions. Having said goodbye to Hickam AFB, Pearl Harbor, Diamond Head and all of the other fascinating places I had the privilege of seeing, I boarded the plane to Maui. Once there, I assumed that Pastor Rugwell would meet me at the airport, but somehow, we got our signals mixed and I wound up being alone, without knowing anyone. I noticed that the stores in the mezzanine were pulling down the metal doors that protected their establishments and thought: "Boy, what do I do now?", since Brother Rugwell did not answer my phone call I made to him upon arrival. Since there were still a restaurant or two that were open, I decided to go in and buy something to eat before they closed their doors too, supposing that afterwards, I would just have to sleep on my luggage bags until the next morning. Besides, the mosquitoes seemed to be eating me alive as I waited there in the open air. So, I drug my luggage with me into the restaurant, which had to have seemed strange to the few people who were there. I picked up a tray and picked out the food that I wanted, sort of like buffet style, and went to the cashier, who was a young Hawaiian man, like myself. Strangely enough, even though I was in a foreign place and did not know a soul, I was not worried about a thing because as the scriptures say there was a peace which came over me that "…surpasseth all understanding…" Philippians 4:7 (KJV). For no reason at all, I started whistling the chorus to that great Christian hymn: "Are you washed in the blood?" As I approached the cashier and he heard me whistling, he finished whistling the latter verse of the chorus, in perfect unison with me. We both looked at each other and laughed out loud. I knew only a fellow Christian would know that song. He said: "Praise the Lord Brother! We shook hands vigorously as he asked me: "What's your name?" Pleasantly shocked, I told him. He asked me where I was from and what I was doing here. (There obviously weren't many blacks who came through there I assumed.) I told him everything and my purpose in being there. As I took out the money from my wallet to pay for the food, he wouldn't let me and said he wanted to pay for it! "Wow!" I thought. He doesn't even know me and he's offering to pay for my food? As soon as he could and there were no more customers, he enthusiastically came to my table and we talked and fellowshipped until closing time. He saw that I had nowhere to go and he said: "Would you like to come to my home and stay with me tonight until Pastor Rugwell can come and get you in the morning? "Why, you bet I would", I told him. We wound up at his house where I not only met his beautiful sister, mother and father and but I believe everyone in the household. Who could have guessed that just by whistling a simply, time-honored hymn like "Are you washed in the blood", such provision could be provided? More profoundly, God's Holy Spirit was stirring my spirit to know that if I would not be ashamed of Him, He would never be ashamed of me. (Mark 8:38 (KJV) He also taught me that if I sought first the kingdom of God and his righteousness, he would provide me with all material things necessary to my functioning, even to the point of thriving. Matt 6:30-34 (KJV). Throughout the years, I have tried very hard to remember that, for without Him, where would we be?

The next day, Pastor Rugwell did indeed show up. He apologized for the misunderstanding but I assured him that even his not coming to pick me up was in God's plan. He asked how and I explained to him that had it not been for the mix up, I never would have met the wonderful Christian Hawaiian family that so graciously took me into their home, without even knowing who I was. That to me, was a blessing that I will never forget, as the reader can plainly see. Brother Rugwell smiled and took me home and to his church. I enjoyed the congregation, though a bit smaller than the one in Pearl City. The brethren were very lovable, mostly older and full of wisdom, which was something a 23 year old man sorely needed. Though my stay with Pastor Rugwell was only a few weeks long, I learned lessons during that time that have stayed with me throughout my Christian walk. Also, a beautiful elderly lady of Portuguese descent named Rosa, for some reason took to me and I to her. I loved to just sit on her porch and listen to her tell me stories of her family, how she arrived in Hawaii and her story of conversion to Christianity. When it came time to leave, I was sad to go, but to my surprise, she had hand knitted a long knitted men's shawl for me, complete with a hood! I was so taken aback, that a hug and a heart-felt thank you did not seem like enough. How much did her hand-knitted work mean to me? It has been almost 40 years and I still have it in my closet to this day. I loved Rosa and someday hope to see her in heaven because I know she is there. God bless her memory.

This long knitted tunic with hood is what sister Rosa Caravalho made for me upon my departure from Wainanalo. I loved that sister so much that even after 40 years, I still retain her gift to me in good condition. It is my way of paying homage to her and the love she showed me.

What the brethren in Maui showed me more than anything else was that whether you belong to an older generation or a younger one, we are truly bound to one another by the love of Christ. They never let the fact that they were older stand in their way of seeing my God-given potential. In fact, one of the reasons Pastor Rugwell wanted me to come there was to help him in the music department until other brethren could arrive and I was more than glad to do that. As far as the practical sides of things go, there were cows outside of the pastor's quarters for instance and at times, I would have to go in to retrieve something or other from the small barn that was on the other side of the cow pasture. I learned that you have to be careful around cow dung, otherwise you might slip on it and fall, which I did. It was alright though, because I had never really lived in the country so it was another fascinating part of my adventure, as I called it. I was able to go with the pastor to see black sand beaches found only on Waimanalo and Kona, which held me in awe. We, along with other tourists, walked over a small bridge and while on the bridge, in the middle, someone gave me a rock and asked me to just let it fall over the black abyss upon which the bridge spanned. I did and never heard a sound. That scared me a little and I hurried up off the bridge. I thought: "Boy, if anyone wanted to take a fast track to hell, I guess this would be the way." There was also green hills to observe, the laid back island style of the people and cultural mix of ethnicities, which really opened my eyes to the possibility of living in harmony among each other, though we all are different. They so impacted me that I decided to see God's potential in everyone I would meet, whether Christian or not. Perhaps I was naïve, but sometimes I think it is better that way because of the negative views and opinions of the world and if we as Christians are not careful, we can also allow such negative influences to affect those who are in their "first love" with Christ. Believe me, I was in my first love back then. Thus, I hugged Pastor Rugwell and thanked him for all his hospitality, promised to keep in touch and boarded the plane for stateside. Next stop? (Barring layovers) Massachusetts and my father and sisters who were anxious to see me again. This time however, the young man that returned was totally different than the one that left. To my surprise, lo and behold, so was he.

Chapter 3

My dad picked me up at Bradley International Airport in Windsor Locks, CT. He arrived in a fairly new Montego MX. I know because it was my car and just before I shipped out to Hawaii, I drove it home so that he could keep it for me until I returned. We hugged each other and I had to admit, I had his smile. Needless to say, he was proud of his son and we chatted about how things had changed and what my plans were. The house on Dartmouth Street was humungous, compared to the places we used to live. An old quintessential 13-room New England colonial revival style home, it appeared a little imposing. It was green on the outside and had a spacious side and back yard. It still needed work but daddy was pretty handy at doing in-home repairs and I even helped him put in a new kitchen floor later on. Families were typically large during those earlier decades and I knew daddy had bought it when this in mind along with the idea of fixing it up and housing all of his children so that everyone could have their own room or at the very least, not argue about using the bathroom. There were three bathrooms in that house. We pulled up in the long driveway and I took my luggage up to my room. Because it was such an old home, it needed many repairs and over time, my sisters and I would be tasked to help in certain major repairs, such as replacing old wallpapers. As I mentioned, I helped redo our kitchen floor and fix up the basement. My eldest sister never lived in the house because she had gotten married already since the time I had been in the military. We were all returning either from Alabama or Ohio to what my father hoped was a more stable environment. As it turned out, none of us stayed there any great length of time because we were all older and everyone began to seek after his or her dream. As time went by though, my sisters eventually moved out and went on with their lives and it was basically my youngest brother and myself, so we did the best we could trying to maintain the place. After a while, even my youngest brother left as well, and became a pretty good cook.

Despite all of these things happening, I noticed that my father had "changed" drastically. He no longer drank, swore and regularly attended church with his third wife. He loved to work with children and developed a children's choir in the Baptist church he attended. This was a pleasant change. He thanked me for the use of my car for the two plus years I had been absent. He also noticed the drastic change in me and from time to time, I would accompany him to his church functions and activities. Nevertheless, since he loved the Baptist doctrine and I had embraced the Pentecostal doctrine, I decided to seek out those of likeminded faith, but I felt the Holy Spirit tug to do it amongst the Spanish-speaking population. I also had felt a strong urge to connect with some of the friends I had known in times past. The first of course, was Butchy but I found out that he indeed, had gone into the service after all, just not with me, as he had promised. I asked his mother if she could do me a favor and let him know that I was searching for him and to contact me as soon as he was able. He never did. Secondly, I sought out my favorite Spanish-speaking high school friends, some of whom had also married or secured work with regional companies. However, one of my best friends who was on equal footing in friendship with Butchy (even moreso because we were so close that he invited me to go with him to Puerto Rico, meet more of his extended family and learn more Spanish and I did) was Francisco Gomez. Even though initially I was very happy to see him again, now he had shacked up with some American girl and even had a child with her, which totally shocked me because he was not prone to do something like that before. To me, it seemed as though his life had taken a turn towards an unhealthy lifestyle, which did not exclude drug use, profanity and a liberal attitude towards carnality. (Look who is speaking about a carnal lifestyle?) Even though I liked and appreciated him, I felt disturbed in my spirit and knew that sadly, we probably wouldn't be seeing much of each other again.

Since, my newly embraced denomination was with the Assemblies of God, I sought them out, only this time a Spanish-speaking one. I quickly located a church not too far the house on Dartmouth Street. At first, it appeared as though the people there seemed suspicious of me, as it was not common for an African- American to seek fellowship with them nor did they seek it outside of their ethnicity. But there were a few people I had met while there who it seemed were not prone to inhibitions and suspicions. I knew by this time that every race has its good and evil people, but that doesn't necessarily mean we should stereotype the whole race for a few bad apples.

Another person who stood out as a good brother in Christ and friend was a young man named Jose Claudio. Even to this day when I think about him, he stands out as an exceptional person who let his love show and never flinched an inch regarding the subject of backing my desire for fellowship and friendship. It was he who showed me the inside of the church, introduced me every week to different brethren, starting with the pastor, then the congregation members and even his own mother and brother, all of whom became accepting of me as time went by. I suppose my progress was steady because after about a year or two, the pastor began giving me small projects to do, I believe just to see how I would fare out in them. The name of the church janitor at that time was Julian and I loved helping him do small projects when I could and had the time. He was a very talented man who could fix just about anything. I also loved tithing from my salary as this was something that I understood God commanded us to do from his word.

The pastor also noted that and when I joined the youth society, he gave me even more responsibilities, including preaching in front of the whole congregation from time to time, which at first terrified me, but later on become second nature. I became a bus driver for the church and held that position for 9 years. Prior to this though, the pastor, seeing my zeal for the things of God, encouraged me to attend bible institute in Hartford, Ct, which I did for 3 years and completed the program. I found that just being busy in and of itself does not edify the spirit, but rather is usually an excuse for a more serious underlying problem. Business just makes one tire, not more spiritual. In fact, it tends to detract from it if we're not careful. During all this time, the "sin" that easily beset me never entered the picture, nor did the thought of succumbing to masturbation for years because I constantly kept myself busy in the Lord's work. But when I started to become lax in the spiritual areas of importance, such as fasting, praying, reading the word of God and participating in edifying church activities, that is when my mind began to entertain these thoughts. The places of employment where I found work at did not pay the best, but it was enough to take care of my needs and help out my dad with the rent and other things at the house.

When I sought employment elsewhere because of dissatisfaction, those Jobs never seemed to be the right "fit", so I would never stay with them very long, especially the salesman profession. Then the bright idea came to me that I should do what my father did, which was become an over-the-road long or short distance truck driver. I also decided to join the Air Force Reserves too, to increase my income. These activities were not necessarily bad in and of themselves, but they became the reasons why I began to spend less and less time in communion with God, the brethren at the church and other spiritual endeavors which keep believers from falling into diverse temptation. In a nutshell, I became negligent and as such, began to show signs of a weakening resolve to resist the devil's devices.

I eventually obtained my Class A license, as they were called in those days, and obtained employment with a trucking company that paid pretty decently and certainly much more than those salesman jobs I had. The drawback was that the job afforded me less and less time in the church and those activities which keep our spirits vigilant against the wiles of the enemy. Couple that with the fact that I would be gone for entire weekends when I had to fulfill my Air Force reserve active duty days and it wasn't long before "cracks" started to appear in my Christian armor, as it were. Truck stops were full of those same dirty, licentious magazines that I had once thrown away in Hawaii, and curiosity got the best of me so from time to time, I would glance through them. I knew it certainly wasn't to read anything interesting in them, but rather to look at the naked women. The Holy Spirit convicted me of that right away and I knew it was wrong. Trying to quell His convicting power is futile, but I tried to. As far as I can pinpoint, that is where from I sporadically began to masturbate, fantasizing over the images presented in those magazines. I felt absolutely horrible, and moreso when in town because I would keep up the façade of being such a spiritual believer, while in the background, I had let corruptive influences infiltrate me. I do not know if anyone caught on, but I know God and I knew what I was doing was wrong. The dilemma was I knew absolutely no one who I could confide in enough to confess this sin. I wound up going to a psychiatrist in Springfield hospital. I cried like a baby about what I was doing. Strangely enough, he said that such conduct was more normal than I thought for young men to exhibit that type of behavior when dealing with sexual matters and excused it as not being as serious as I was making it out to be. I quickly corrected him and quoted bible verses to prove that I indeed should not be doing these things. (He obviously wasn't a Christian) He countered with some bible verses of his own, but he misquoted one in the Old Testament, which I quickly corrected and he praised me for my bible knowledge. I told him my bible knowledge was to no avail if I continued doing what I was, because I would probably wind up in hell. He thought that was a bit drastic, but nevertheless, prescribed me some powerful drugs which would affect my libido so that even if I wanted to do something, I probably wouldn't be able to and he scheduled me for another three appointments with him. I was so embarrassed that I never went back. Those episodes were short-lived and I got back on track without anyone being the wiser, but I felt sad that I had let myself and others down, even though they knew nothing about this pernicious addiction. I will admit that fasting always seemed to help me out and I remember doing 7 days without food and water and many 3-day ones as well. I don't share that to be pompous, but rather to show that even those measures are fruitless *if* the root problem is not addressed. The fact that I eventually fell back into this unacceptable behavior proves that if the base desire to defeat the vice is absent, no matter what the vice may be, all the fasting, crying and praying in the world will be of no discernible avail. Then, as now, I can declare that within me I find no good thing. The only worthy thing is Christ in me, and that only by his grace. But

I am thankful that our God is so merciful. If that were not a fact, this abbreviated testimony would have never been written.

I can say however, that the best highlight of my experience while attending the Spanish Assemblies of God was meeting my beloved wife, Lucy. When I met her, she had never been married but had two small children and I thought she looked so attractive with her two small boys in tow. I saw in her a woman who despite her circumstances, was willing to give all to God and let him lead her. Plus she was cute too. We gradually got to know one another and believe it or not, within six months we were married. Now I know that seems pretty extreme to some and many would say that there needed to be more time to know one another, but when God is in the matter, he takes care of details like that. I can't thank the Lord enough that he blessed me with her, because it has been over 33 years now (34 in September) and we love each other more today, than we did then. I got along great with my stepsons, Javier and Marcus and raised them just like they were my own because when there is true love, there really shouldn't be any distinction. Marcus, my youngest followed me into military service and went on to obtain two bachelor degrees and is currently working on his master's degree. Javier, my eldest secured a great job with excellent pay in Connecticut and is slowly moving up the chain of responsibility at his own pace. They also turned out to be responsible fathers to their children and always honor their mother. Even though they are not serving the Lord as we would like to see them, they tell us they will never forget their Christian upbringing and for us to never give up on them and to keep them in our prayers, which of course we always will.

After being with the church for about 10 years or so, I decided to rejoin the military full time because I did not like the fact that the trucking industry was taking so much time away from my family and church, plus I already knew that you automatically get 30 days leave in the military. (When you get to take it is another story altogether) It was not easy saying goodbye to all the wonderful brothers and sisters I had come to love because they had become a part of my life. My father on the other hand, understood because he himself was a veteran of WWII and had seen how the Lord was blessing me, despite all the inconsistencies in my life. He never knew of my moral problems either. I promised to keep in touch as much I could. Likewise, as you might expect after having been in Springfield for many years, my wife and children found it a little difficult to adjust to the idea in the beginning but, after a while they came to accept it and were even a little excited about moving to another state and meeting new people. Even though I was Air Force all the way, when I went to rejoin the active force full time, they told me I would have to wait a full year, which I was not willing to do because I was tired of being in Springfield. So, the Air Force recruiter suggested that if I really wanted to get out fast, just join the Army and I would be gone before I knew it. Looking back now, there was no way I could not have been thinking rationally, because if I had, I would never have done it, but for some reason, I thought that was a good idea, so I did it.

I rejoined at a Meps station in Connecticut and went through basic training a second time in Fort Dix, New Jersey. My dad, his and my wife came and my boys came to see me at my graduation. Then I headed to Aberdeen Proving Grounds, Maryland for special training in my military occupation specialty. Afterwards, I received orders to go to Fort Riley, Kansas, where my dad was kind enough to drive my wife and kids all the way from Massachusetts to there. We found a home in Manhattan, Kansas and eventually wound up buying it. Though it was humble, we called it our own and were proud of it. We registered the boys in the local schools (because Javier was 5 years older than his brother, which necessitated them having to go to two different schools) and after a while, they began to make friends. We found the worship services on the base to be quite dry and lackluster, so we opted to seek out the type we were used to back in the northeast. Try as we may though, there were no Assemblies of God churches in the immediate area, so we found one with similar beliefs in Junction City, Kansas and tried as best we could to become a part of the congregation.

Actually, it was through friends and acquaintances made during our time at the Fort Riley that we became familiar with the area churches.

The first one we went to was a small one with loveable church members and we got to know them all. My specialty kept me in the field quite a bit though, and if that were not the case, then there were interval military training and other activities which also consumed quite a bit of time. My wife was a good woman and pitched in to help as much as she could to make our house a home. Kansas winters can be brutal and the church we attended was about a half an hour from our home in Manhattan. Just the same, she would brave the distance and take the children with her to church. Nonetheless, an incident occurred which affected the church and it went through a split and another group was formed. This saddened us as we weren't aware of any dissention which might cause this and to us, the pastor was a humble, God-fearing man. Faced with a decision we really did not want to make, we went with our friends from the Fort to the new church and they even wanted my wife to become the pastor of the church after a while. After submitting the matter to God in prayer, she accepted but found out that there were certain people within the church that were disapproving of her being their leader and made it difficult for her to fully function as well as she would have liked to. She eventually decided to leave. It just so happened that right around this time I also received orders to go to South Korea. That was a bombshell because it usually was a yearlong isolated tour, which meant I had to go alone and family members were not allowed come. Since most of the people in the church were military, they were used to seeing people come and go but this was all new to us. Anyway, we said our goodbyes and I headed out to Korea and my wife and kids stayed there and "held the fort down", as they say, at least for a while (No pun intended). My wife was well known in Springfield and as an E-4 our income just barely allowed us to cover the mortgage payments and grocery bills with not much left over. It was then she suggested: Why not temporarily return to Springfield and fill an open job slot just waiting for her until my tour in Korea ended? It turned out to be a good idea because it was then that the Gulf War started and instead of a year,

Airman First Class Michael Wright (1973- 77)

I had to stay 14 months in Korea. She, on the other hand made enough money where we could keep up payments with the house and the boys were happy to see their old friends again, even if it was just on a temporary basis.

Korea was a tough place to be but there were thousands of soldiers spread throughout the peninsula. It just so happened that because of my specialty, I was shipped up north to Camp Casey, 2nd I.D. Everyone knew that if the North Koreans ever invaded the South, we would all but be decimated because they had about a million-man army amassed on the border. In effect, for them we were just a "speed bump" on the way to South Korea. I tried to settle in as best I could with the routine and I suppose I didn't do too bad of a job. I was a Chemical Weapons NCO and Squad leader. While there, I was promoted to E-5 or sergeant. What little after work time I had was spent with the Amer-asian orphanages or in the on-base chapels, which were not too distant one from another. However, they were times when again, I would "slip" and fall into that damnable vice which of course would leave me feeling horrible about myself and send me into a deep depression. I saw how isolation and loneliness affected many of my fellow soldiers. All dealt with it in various ways. Some would occupy their time in extracurricular sports activities or lift weights in the gym or go on post-sponsored tours to downtown Seoul. Others, like myself, would try and seek Christian fellowship or I would just stay in my room and write letters to everyone I knew, especially my wife. She received a letter from me every week and sometimes two. As a squad leader, even though one has personal problems, the sergeant must put those aside to attend to the wellbeing of his soldiers. This I did with great pride. But the greatest activity for the Christian should be the time of fellowship he spends with his Lord and Savior, whether it be in the morning, noon or evening. Whenever I did this, things would go great. When I did not, temptation would beckon me and I would not always resist. Even though I would never think about sleeping with another woman given my marriage vows, there was one time when I foolishly let one of the area prostitutes do to me what I knew should never be done. For this extreme lack of spiritual judgment and carnal failure, I cried for days on end and had to eventually confess it to my wife when I went to see her on leave. Needless to say, she was devastated by this, angry and found it quite hard to forgive me. I certainly could not blame her and knew she had every right to be incensed with me. Nevertheless, in time we did reconcile and I promised her that the rest of my tour would be spent in my room and with the orphans or other Christians, and that was it. That is exactly what I did. God allowed me to fulfill those words and we were happy to see each other and my boys when the tour finally ended. By this time, my boys were becoming used to being enrolled or un-enrolled in schools. They maintained fairly decent grades and if there were any subjects which gave them problems, we tried to help them to understand the subjects. They were always amongst other military kids, so that helped them transition a little smoother than if they never had anyone to relate to. On my way back from Korea, I attempted to change my military specialty (96D—Photo Analyst of Top Secret Sensitive Material) thinking that it might help out my career. That move obligated me to take a temporary detour to Fort Huachuca, Arizona. That however, did not seem to be in God's plans and therefore, did not work out as I had expected. It was at this point that we received orders to go to Fort Carson, Colorado. This anticipated move made us excited because my sister lived in Denver, Colorado with her family so the prospect of seeing her again and new adventures made us more ready to think positively about our future. I was able to sell our house in Manhattan and even made a small profit.

Before we knew it, we were settling in on-post housing in Colorado Springs, Colorado with the 4th I.D. We quickly settled into our new routine and the boys made friends quicker this time. I was introduced to my unit, met my chain of command and again was designated a squad leader. Because the battalion commander needed a hard-charging individual, he canvassed the companies to find out if any of the NCOs would be willing to go to Indianapolis, Indiana to Master Fitness School and fulfill those requirements. I volunteered as soon as I heard because I loved to do activities involving physical fitness. Boy, did I almost bite off more than I could chew. Master Fitness School was quite hard, but by God's grace,

I did very well. When I returned, I received a certificate of appreciation from the battalion commander. Nevertheless, this new addition to my growing list of small accomplishments keep me busier than I expected. Since the other companies did not have a master fitness trainer, they asked my First Sergeant if they could "borrow" me and he was always happy to oblige, whether I wanted to or not, if you know what I mean. That meant that I did not always get home in time for dinner but my wife took it in stride, like the good trooper she was. She also was not content to just sit around doing nothing, but rather she began to actively seek and find a good job that generated a decent income for our family. Pretty much anything my wife put her mind to do, she would accomplish it and always gave God the glory for it. We again, found that it was easier for us to adapt to churches outside in the local area, as opposed to inside because of the ecumenical spirit that pervades many of the post chapels and the pervasive disdain for the use of the word "Jesus" in Christian worship services. This, mind you, in a nation founded on Christian principles. This we found to be very hypocritical and fueled our suspicions that someone at a higher echelon was trying to control what could and could not be preached, and that did not sit well with us then, nor does it today.

We eventually found an Assemblies of God church and attended there faithfully, involving ourselves with the faith community there. That lasted about 2 years or so, but then we noticed that everything was run by the pastor and his family, including the treasury funds and pretty much all aspects of the church. This is not necessarily all bad, as long as there are checks and balances in place in order to avoid abuse, excesses or unaccountability. It was as though there were no other people qualified to pitch in and help, but they did not appear to want anyone else to get involved in the finances. Now please understand, these were wonderful, amiable folks and it was easy to see that Joe Malacara (That was the pastor's name) had a great vision and a love for the lost. It was just in this area of finances, it appeared that discrepancies were noted. I of course, loved to be involved in the music department and volunteered my time and talents towards that end. I would help out in Sunday school, as would my wife when asked. Our boys, who had become young men about this time, would accompany us and meet new Christian acquaintances. We raised them with as much Christian admonition exposure and training as we could give them, not only in church but more importantly, at home and at the kitchen table.

Praying as a family before going to bed was something we loved to do whenever opportunity afforded itself. Nevertheless, we were aware that the boys were only human and were affected by worldly influence just like anyone else. We quickly realized that if we did not correct for those influences in a timely fashion, they could wind up splintering the household and causing irreparable spiritual and emotional damage. So we did, but with love and firmness and singleness of purpose.

It was around this time that we were invited to attend another area church, (although not Assemblies of God) by another brother who had previously been with us where we were currently attending. It was on a day when we didn't have service, so I told my wife I would go first and check it out to see how it was. Turned out, the church and the people were fine. The denomination happened to be Church of God, Cleveland Tennessee. The pastor's name was Roy and he was very nice, as was his wife. Back at our church, there was an investigation by the higher ups of the church finances and it was never made clear if there were some misappropriations of funds or not, but we decided that it was time to make a change. So, we once again said our goodbyes to the good folks there and headed over to "Roy's" church. We slowly settled into the routine and I was linked with the music ministry, which happened to be very good in that church. The boys, once again made new acquaintances as did my wife, especially among Spanish-speaking attendees. I cannot recall being affected by or succumbing to "the vice" (viewing pornography) too much while in Colorado. Thank God that constant involvement in Christian and military activities really left no time for any shenanigans. Because my wife and I both loved to minister, we were blessed to make acquaintances with Frank & Betty, a wonderful Christian couple who ministered in the prisons through Chuck Colson's prison ministries. I loved ministering to the prisoners and traveling down to Canon City and my wife and Betty would frequent the women's prison in Pueblo, Colorado. On special occasions, we were allowed to give joint services (prison officials allowed men in to minister with the women) where I could come in along with the ladies and be part of a special guest program and minister. Our eyes were truly opened as to the need in these places and the great lack of ministers or Christian lay people willing to go behind bars. So, at every opportunity, we went through the courses and received certificates which allowed us to exercise that ministry. That is something that we did throughout our time in Colorado and keep doing to this very day, although the ministry has been expanded. We also travelled on short missionary jaunts to the cross-border towns and cities in Mexico on at least three different occasions. We have always been a people of humble means, so to stay with our fellow Mexican pastors in their humble abodes was no big deal. Some of those who travelled with us could not stomach the none-running toilets, the cockroaches crawling up the wall and sometime in the food or the shanty-like dwellings found in the neighborhood, but I asked within myself: "Then why did you come, since you knew that you would encounter situations like this?" Was not the very idea to minster to the poor and those who lack the things we take for granted? Those trips showed us how spoiled some of us are, even in the Christian community. God forbid that some of them should ever lose their material possessions because I don't think they would make it. In any case, it was truly a blessing to see these beautiful brethren accept with great gratitude the clothes and financial support we brought to them. We preached and ministered in the churches in Juarez, met dedicated people from other countries who had ministered for years and decades in ministry. In fact, one of the pastors we stayed with was actually Honduran, but had been in Mexico so long, that he obtained his Mexican citizenship there. Another pastor was from Puerto Rico but he had lived there 25 years and his wife was of course, Mexican. You wouldn't really have known that he was Puerto Rican unless he revealed his accent. We were blessed to be part of such experiences.

My two young boys were quickly growing into two young men and the eldest had finished high school. They both were active in sports activity and while only 17 years old, my eldest took state champions in

Sargent Wright attending BNCOC at Aberdeen Proving Grounds, MD
(SGT Wright is seen in the 3rd line standing, (R to L) at the extreme right.)

squatting at 505 lbs., a record for that year. We cheered them on at just about every football game they had. Upon graduation, I had suggested some Christian colleges that he might want to attend but in the end, he chose to go to Liberty University in Lynchburg, Virginia. My wife was not too keen on him going so far away from home but I was praying that the Christian college experience would deepen his love and zeal for the things of God. Little did I know that just the opposite would happen. So, he kissed his mom goodbye, hugged his brother, said goodbye to his friends and we both headed out for Virginia. Javy drove his car, following me in mine because once there, I had to return and help my family prepare for the move. Everything seemed to be going quite well and then out of the blue, guess what I received? Orders to go overseas. Where? To my shock and horror, South Korea a second time! I cannot tell you how much I raised the roof and tried to get out of going on another isolated tour, especially knowing what I went through the last time. But, it was to no avail. This time though, my wife and son took it much better than the first time.

Arriving at Kim Po Airport, everything was familiar to me. I again was sent to Camp Casey, 2nd I.D. I fell into the routine much easier this time and was eventually promoted to E-6. I naturally gravitated to the children's orphanages in my spare time. I also visited Dr. David Yonggi Cho's famous church. I was even chosen to be an interim pastor of a small church of soldiers of all ranks, where we met outside of Camp Casey in the small town of Dong Du Chon. I met wonderful dedicated Christian students and even introduced a good Christian Amer-asian brother and friend to a nice girl who later on became his wife. My communication with my wife was constant and when the six month mark came up, I was more than happy to take my leave and be with her and Marcus, my youngest. Shortly after my return to Korea, I found out that my son had suddenly returned home from Liberty University, totally dejected and disgusted. Taken aback, I asked him what happened. He told me that despite the fact that Liberty was touted as a Christian university, he ran into open racism and bigotry, beginning with his own roommate, who it appears harbored deep-seated racist attitudes against African-Americans.

Of course, his father was one so my son wasn't going to take that lying down. He did not realize that many parents, having failed to do a good job of raising their children with morals, boundaries and Christian ethics, simply cart them off to these universities. They hope that that faculty and interaction will do what they failed to, which is instill value, respect for one another no matter what ethnicity and encourage a personal salvation experience with Christ. He said his coach really liked him and would guarantee him a slot on the football team. He did start attending practices there and liked the coach and it sounded like there was still hope. But the student loans he had taken out did not arrive in time for some of the necessary core courses he had to take. Even though I had left him my credit card to take care of anything he might need, he felt it would be hard for him to catch up if he did not start with his class on time. So all of these things combined to discourage him and in the end, he decided to return home. I was very saddened at this turn of events but encouraged him to have faith in God and maybe something better would come out of it. There was little I could do, being so far away. It was a frustrating time for both my wife and I. My wife later told me that some of my son's friend in Fort Carson were influencing him negatively and she did not like it and made it clear to Javy. So, in order to avoid more conflict, my son decided that he would return to Massachusetts, where he was more familiar and live with one of his cousins there. My wife's *objections* to this were *well founded* because once he settled in there, his conduct degenerated and soon he was smoking, got tattoos, began to wear earrings and use profanity and began living with a girlfriend he had met, and not necessarily in that order. One thing was certain though, he was no longer interested in attending church or even the things of God. That broke our hearts because we felt as though we had miserably failed in our mission to bring up boys to love the Lord. In Korea, I cried when alone in my room. Soon though, my time was up and once again was reunited with my wonderful wife. The remainder of our time at Fort Carson flew by and before we knew it, we received orders to go to Fort Stewart, Georgia.

Chapter 4

The moving vans arrived and in familiar fashion, boxed up all of our belonging and we found ourselves in Hinesville, Georgia. I should mention that since joining the Army, no matter where I was stationed, there is a place called the National Training Center in Fort Irwin California, or NTC for short, which almost all soldiers and marines go to in order to train in case we have to fight in desert terrains. My count of having gone there by the time I arrived at Fort Stewart, Georgia was 6 or 7. Nevertheless, a great highlight to arriving in Georgia was that we were able to purchase our first new home. It was a surreal experience for us because up until that point, I never owned anything new, except the new car I had bought for myself when I first enlisted in the Air Force. To see the moving vans arrive and the workers unpack our belonging and put them into our new home was very gratifying, to say the least. I was not scared of a 30-year fixed mortgage because I always knew I would never take that long to pay it off. I now know it wasn't as easy as I thought it would be. Anyway, I settled into my new unit, met my chain of command and began the now familiar routine of early morning risings and late evening dinners with my family. Marcus, my youngest seemed to settle well in school and did equally well in his studies. We talked telephonically with Javy, my oldest and encouraged him to repent and seek God's best for his life. We found a local church with the Pentecostal Church of God, International Mission. The pastor of this church was a women and dedicated servant of the Lord. We felt that for the moment, this is where we could help make a difference, as it was a small church and could use our help. We became familiar with the folks who attended and soon were helping in different church activities including singing, playing instruments, preaching and doing sporadic evangelism. My youngest also met friends his age, although some of the adolescents and young adults who were in church were there simply because their parents brought them there and not necessarily because they were saved and Christian. This of course is a common practice worldwide, because children must go where their parents take them and submit to their rules until such time as they are mature enough to make their own decisions. Was it not the same with me? At this point though, we were glad to be involved in Christian activity where people could be helped. My wife, who always involved in church activities found out about an opportunity to travel to a foreign country through contacts made with a Spanish ministry called "Cristo Viene" through the international Evangelist Yiye Avila. It was an opportunity for her to go to India in order to help out the poor and get to know certain pastors, while there. I also attempted to accompany my wife, but because of the sensitivity of military issues and the inability to guarantee my protection if I were to travel there, I was not allowed to go because I was still a G.I., you know a government issue, as we soldiers were nicknamed. So, after praying and leaving all in God's hands, I paid for her trip there and back and sent her on her way while the boys and I continued our routine at home. It was a time of great learning for her. She went to the Madras region to a place called 'Malacapari' and there she met with an engaging, humble pastor by the name of Spurgeon Babu. She preached to multitudes of people but she also became sick for 3 days because of the rainy season there. She experienced 'culture shock', (seeing cows run free in the streets while people were starving) and understood better the plight of the poor in a caste society. Upon her return from there, she was still sick for a week but eventually recovered. She learned more and more what it was to step out in faith and trust in God. To this day, she still receives email communications with Pastor Babu and we pray for him and thousands of other dedicated ministers who give their lives to the Lord's work every day in India.

It was in one of the later years during my stay in Georgia (a total of 4) that I began to become lax in my spiritual vigilance and as a result, once again began yielding to sporadic episodes of viewing pornography and occasional masturbation. There was no excuse for this so the guilt that I felt after doing these things was debilitating but apparently not

Michael and Lucy's wedding photo with his father and his wife Mary Anne
(seen at the extreme right, same row), his step-brother Steve, and Lino and
Miriam Maldonado and one of the daughters of our friend, Faith (1982)

Michael and Lucy in the beginning years of their
marriage with Javier (6) and Marcus, (3) at that time.

An article about mixed families appeared in the
local newspaper (1992-Sunday Republican)

Family Reunion. Lowest first row, Javier is seen at the extreme right when he was only 6 years old. Second row, Lucy is seen, second from L to R, the second person. Third row, L to R, Michael is seen and his father in in the same row at the extreme right holding his grandson, Marcus, who was only 3 years old at the time. They say that my father and I have the same smile. Do you believe that? Do they have a point?

enough to make me stop. On one occasion during these episodes in our home, my wife walked in on me in our bathroom and caught me. She was totally shocked and extremely mad at me for doing this, not to mention insulted. I told her that the problem lied with me and not with her, confessing that I had this problem since before knowing her, even as an adolescent. She eventually came around and forgave me but this incident but I knew from within that I needed to try and get a handle on the situation before an even a worse fate or encounter might await me. The blame for this conduct has always lied squarely on my shoulders and it has always been a case of me letting my spiritual guards down and whenever that has happened, heartbreak, deceit, lies and dishonesty occurs. In short, I open the door to fruits of the flesh, when Galatians 5:19-21(KJV) warns of what happens to those who allow those things to happen. Verses 22-24 exhort believers to manifest the fruit of the spirit. Had I done this, I probably would not be writing about these blatant failures. I prayed and cried about this fault and hoped that God would see me through and give me the strength to overcome it.

Around this time, I was in a unit that I liked but one day, I received orders to prepare for another isolated tour, only this time it was to Southeast Asia, to the tiny nation-state of Qatar. I never even heard of such a place, so I had to investigate where exactly it was on a world map I had, and found it was a gulf state, as it is known, next door to Saudi Arabia. Again, it was not the first time I had been in this part of the world. As a matter of fact, it was the 3rd time since the first two times were army exercises of short tours of about 4 months and 8 months respectively. On the first tour, I was blessed enough to be able to work with different armies of the world in a joint military exercise testing how various armies worked and coordinated together during wartime, using simulated scenarios. We were in Egypt, in the Sinai desert. One morning, our captain asked if there was anyone who wanted to go and see the pyramids of Egypt. A bunch of us jumped up and raised our hands. Are you kidding? When would we ever be able to see something like that again in our lives? So, we dressed in civilian clothes, mounted a bus and away we went. Believe it or not, I remember standing in line along with

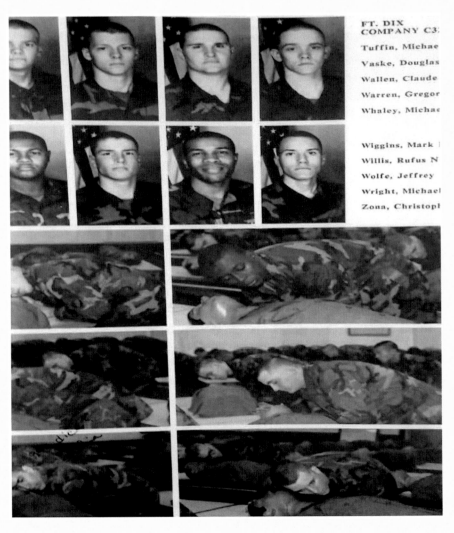

FT. DIX
COMPANY C3:

Tuffin, Michae
Vaske, Douglas
Wallen, Claude
Warren, Gregor
Whaley, Michae

Wiggins, Mark
Willis, Rufus N
Wolfe, Jeffrey
Wright, Michael
Zona, Christopl

E-3 Wright graduating from KMY/BAC Training in 1987, Ft. Dix, N.J.

PFC Wright (previous service considered) graduating from Army Basic Training in 1987. (First line standing, 2nd soldier holding the flag. (R to L)

Marcus, his dad, mom and fellow airman enjoying the
Boardwalk in downtown San Antonio, TX. (2000)

Marcus today, at 34.

many people, mostly foreign from various nations. As we neared the point of entry into the tallest pyramid, I happened to be number 250. After I entered, the guard at the entrance placed a rope across a banister and said: "No more." What I found out later was that because of the carbon dioxide our bodies release when we exhale, that element is detrimental to the insides of the pyramids and because hundreds of tourists go through there every day, they must limit the amount of people now. In any case, I was completely amazed and enthralled to be able to walk those narrow stairs all the way up the pinnacle of the pyramid. There is a small temple, which is roped off. One can assume that the ancient architects constructed it for astrological purposes but whatever the case may have been, it was a once in a lifetime experience, at least it was for me.

Before I knew it, that all too familiar scene was playing itself out again and there I was boarding a plane and heading out after saying my goodbyes to my wife and son. Upon arrival, my superiors quickly oriented to the way things worked in that part of the world. They then gave me my own personal jeep to be mobile and I began to execute my assigned specialty, which in this case was a Quality Assurance NCO for wheeled and tracked vehicle. The pace of things was quick because we were preparing to go into Iraq again and the moniker for this war was Iraqi Enduring Freedom. As was customary, I would look for fellowship outside the fort or post but in an Islamic country, where was such fellowship? Answer? Just about everywhere, believe it or not. To be sure, the underground church in Qatar, (and other Islamic nations) is thriving but it is because they conduct their activities secretly or clandestinely since as almost everyone knows, persecution is a big problem there. We, who are from other nations, are certainly not bound to adhere to their restrictions, but because of our love for our brethren, we are willing to conform to the way they do things over there.

The marquee, (if you will), of the underground church it appears, is quiet non-conformism or not to be seen at all. This is done by attracting as little attention as possible and it was in this manner that I was privileged to be able to preach in the Nepalese, Filipino, Sri Lankan and Pakistani churches during my tour of duty. May I also interject another interesting

Our grandchildren when they were just babies,
Alaina 1 and Xavier 2 years old respectively.

Our granddaughter Alaina when she was a
baby and now at 15 years of age

aspect of my overseas experience at this point. As I had been a sponsor of a little Philippine girl named Joysie Soriano who I had got to know as a single airman, (while in the Air Force) when she was only 9 years old. At that time, she lived in the Batangas province. This sponsorship, friendship and love lasted more than 26 years. I also got to know her mother Teresita and her father, Benedicto and even when they both passed away, I never abandoned, but tried as best I could to continue to support her financially and emotionally. So now, the prospect of my being able to visit the Philippine churches filled me with joy and an enthusiastic outlook. During my stay there, they helped me communicate with Joysie telephonically and write her in Tagalog and the church I most frequented was the Philippine church. What wonderful relations, friendship and discoveries were made while there. I phoned my wife often to relate to her how life there was so different for believers, how enthusiastic the believers were and how we were even planning to conduct a 3-day evangelistic crusade. However, one day when I called my wife on another occasion, she was crying and I asked her what was the matter. She explained that our youngest son and the youngest daughter of the Pastor of the church we were attending in Hinesville had illicit, unprotected sex together and now she was pregnant. This absolutely devastated my wife, not to mention the pastor of the church we were attending, who was rightfully angry at them both because they did it right in her house. I tried to calm her down but she could not be consoled so easily over this sad turn of events. The fact that the pastor also happened to be a female made it that much worse. I assured her we would deal with it more in-depth when I returned but for the moment we needed to rely on God to help get us through this situation. I asked the brethren in the Al Khor church, (the name of the local Filipino congregation) to keep my family in prayers without going into the messy details, and of course they gladly obliged.

This news left me a little depressed, although I tried to maintain my spiritual composure but it was not easy. I can only recall one time when I yielded to the temptation of masturbation. The accompanying guilt and remorse were by now almost second nature, but the hypocrisy of my actions was ever-present in my mind. I simply hated myself for doing

Marcus Ramirez, 2000

Marcus in a photo with those of his Fleet [Lackland AFB, San Antonio, TX] after completing graduation. Lowest row (L to R, the 7th aviator, holder the fleet flag).

Marcus and his Dad, SSG Wright, posing for a photo in front of one of the various planes on display at Lackland AFB, TX. (2000)

Sergeant Wright, his wife Lucy and their son Marcus, when he graduated from Air Force basic training at Lackland AFB, San Antonio TX.

that so I reasoned that fasting might help me overcome it. In reality, I sometimes deceived myself into thinking that I could use fasting as a means of easing my conscious and thereby show God that at least I was trying to do something about my sin. In any case, God was not fooled. If the truth be told, one's heart must be utterly ready to repent of the sin, weakness or fault and leave it behind. Absent this type of mindset, anyone can see that such a person is a double-minded man and is unstable in all his ways, according to James 1:8 (KJV). That man was me. How then, could I even think about scolding my youngest son? Nevertheless, when I talked to my son, I had no shortage of harsh words for him as to what he had done and how he had hurt and disrespected his mother. I told him once the child was born, not to even think about being an irresponsible father because now that he had done this, he would have to see it through to the end, and I meant it. Needless to say, I was quite angry (at myself for being such a hypocrite) and could hardly contain myself. Not too long after this incident, my youngest son decided to follow my footsteps and join the military. I never pushed them towards the military service nor made either of them feel obligated to do so, but I did point out the benefits of being a military man as opposed to just being a simple civilian, especially when the civilian economy was not doing so well. As I was told when I was a young man; "You will always have a job because there will always be wars to fight." Just the same, I always believed that such a decision should be made with the upmost of thought and contemplation. Marcus was a good worker and prior to this incident, had never really given us any real cause for concern, except for the run-of-the-mill stupid things that young teenage boys whimsically do. He always managed to land a job wherever he applied, but even he could see the benefits he could garner if he made a commitment to the armed services. Among other things, it would be a steady income, money for college and more security for his daughter and my granddaughter, whose name by the way, is Alaina Ramirez. So, we encouraged him to follow his dream and he headed off for basic training at Lackland Air Force Base, San Antonio, Texas. He was now an airman. During my six or seventh month mark in country, I was able to take a 30-day leave and come back to the states. It was then that my wife and I were able to take a trip down to Lackland to see our young man graduate from basic training and head out for Air Force specialty training, which was in Warner Robins, Georgia. My eldest son also wanted to join the marines but the doctors told him his feet were flat and that made him ineligible. So, he managed to secure an excellent job with Hallmark greeting cards in Connecticut. He also gave us a grandson, whom he named Xavier. Both of our grandchildren were beautiful babies, born only one year apart from each other and even though these children were born out of wedlock, we claimed them for the Lord and put our trust in Him that his mercy and goodness would keep them innocent despite the circumstances of their births. We can now say, (after 15 years) that the two have been raised in the admonition of the Lord and know what the truth is. We pray that their encounter with Jesus becomes real and they develop an intimate relation with him. Both my sons have proven to be excellent fathers who intricately involve themselves in their children's lives and activities. Today, they share joint-custody responsibilities with their former partners and maintain an amicable relationship with them, Even though each has moved on with their lives. To our relief, our sons have not totally forgotten their Christian upbringing, thank God.

My tour of duty wound down and we received another unexpected surprise, but this time, it was positive. I was to go straight from Southwest Asia to Luxembourg in Europe. All I had to do was come back and clear the post and turn in my issues. Halleluiah! My wife and I had been wanting to go to Europe for the longest time and finally, orders came through. She was excited to hear the news. Plus the fact that she could now leave the city of Hinesville and distance herself from the negative atmosphere that surrounded her gave her something to look forward to. She smiled a little more each day. She called her sisters and let them know that she was headed for Europe and as expected, they all envied her but she told them that once she was established and settled down, if they had the money to travel to where we were, she would invite them but they never came.

I had to leave early to set things up but assured her I would be waiting at the other end. Unbeknownst to us though, she was slated to travel the very same day the radical Islamists slammed two planes into the World Trade Center in New York. Not only was her flight delayed but she had to travel by bus from city to city until such time as a flight to France could be secured. Once she finally arrived at Charles de Gaulle airport, she was able to transfer to an ongoing connection to Luxembourg. Boy, was I ever glad to see her there! She looked beautiful. We chatted all the way from the airport to our apartment in Bettembourg, but I could see she was fascinated with all things European, especially the language. The official rule in Luxembourg is that in order to live there, one must speak fluently, Luxembourgish, French or German. In those years, I thanked God that I had conscientiously studied French ever since being stationed in Fort Riley, Kansas. I recall that while there, I actually met and befriended a lady, who was from France, whose husband happened to be an African-American soldier. This lady set me straight regarding the foundations of French, verbs, adjectives, nouns, pronouns, present, past and future tense and everything one needs to know in order to function in a French-Speaking society, including writing it well.

When I was in Korea, (of all places), I met another lady who also happened to be from France and she also built upon what my first friend helped me with regarding the French language structure. By the way, these ladies never charged me a cent and always willingly sacrificed their time to help me. God bless them wherever they are. While in Qatar, I took the Army language test and passed it. Surprisingly enough, the Army even began paying me for my language skills. I never thought knowing Spanish and French could get you paid, but God was also showing me how being diligent in a discipline, no matter what it might be, does pay off in the long run. So now, it all seemed to fall into place because I could tell my superiors that I spoke French, but more than that, I could prove it amongst the people. Unfortunately, it still wasn't as easy as you might think. For one thing, the Luxembourgish prefer you speak their language over the others, as you might expect, but if you must speak another, the closet kindred is

Joint Service Ceremony with Luxemburgish officials in
front of General Patton's tomb in Luxembourg.
(2002) SSG Wright is seen standing in the middle.

Luxembourg, Europe

German. Boy! That information wasn't in any handbook I read. So, my wife and I had to go out into the population and find out the hard way that not every native of Luxembourg loved the thought of speaking any language, other than their own, especially since Hitler in W WII tried to force them to speak German and erase their own. I totally understood their underlying resentment. Thank God many of them also spoke English. That helped my wife be able to move around when I had to deploy back to southwest Asia again. But for the meantime, it was fun for us getting to know the city, the culture the people and places. We traveled quite often to Germany, France, Belgium and Holland. My wife was quickly integrated into the military wives community and my superiors were top rate NCOs and professional in every sense of the word.

The officers were equally professional and I can say that it was a genuine undeserved blessing from God that he allowed us to experience that tour to Europe. I again was assigned as a QA inspector of tracked and wheeled vehicles bound for the war, which was Iraqi Freedom. As the war progressed, the colonel asked for volunteers to go into southwest Asia, to camp Arifjan (formally camp Doha) in order to speed up the expedition of war vehicles to the theater. Of course, I raised my hand along with some other NCOs in my unit and once preparations were made, we were on our way. Before all of this happened though, we had already been in Europe for about a year and a half and my wife finally got used to traveling on her own to Germany. We met and made friends and even managed to find a Spanish church outside of a post near Kaiserslautern Germany although the pastor just rented the place and held services there. We had to travel to Bit burg Germany to the Air Force base for our medical care and Landstuhl for matters more serious. Germany is a very green and beautiful place and many soldiers and airmen have opted to live out their lives and raise their children there, having married German women. But as for my wife and I, we just enjoyed the country, friendly people and were amazed at the many ethnicities who now called Germany their home. We even met a young Mexican Christian guitarist who because his wife was German and spoke Spanish fairly well, decided to stay

Fellow soldiers take Sergeant Wright's picture during a rare break in their training, when they were at NTC in California. [1990-92 Fort Riley, KS]

in Germany for the rest of his life. There were also Turkish, Africans, and Russians, Portuguese, even Cubans and other ethnicities, the great majority of whom spoke German very well. Amazing! This certainly cannot be what Hitler envisioned, right? Anyway, by the time the call to go to southwest Asia came around, my wife was confident enough to know how to navigate these places and go wherever she needed to go. While in Luxembourg, my wife happened to secure employment working at the encampment where our main operations were. She made extremely good wages there and I always say it was because God wanted to bless my wife for her constant faithfulness, humbleness and faith. If anyone deserved it, it was her. As far as falling prey to my temptations went? I was not completely free from it but I can say they were extremely curtailed; that is to say, *almost* never did that while there, but I still had work to do.

The months spent in the Southwest Asia Theater seemed to fly by and the pace of the war preparation left little time for much else, but I would share the gospel with the soldiers or officers who were willing to listen. There were also bible studies going on in the tents or after hours in the dinning tents as time would allow. I should also mention that I had tried every way recommended to me to advance to the next rank, which for me was E-7. I went to the schools, did record reviews, visited Ft. Benjamin Harrison, obtained my Associates degree and as I said, tried to do all I knew how to obtain it. It was no use or just not meant to be or it wasn't in God's plans. So, as my 20 years (about 28 if I include my reserve time in the Air Force) was about to come to a close, my chain of command informed me that they would have to pull me back from going to war going on in Iraq and return me to Europe to process out of the military because in order to go over 20 years, one must have the corresponding rank. Lacking this, one must retire.

I truly wanted to follow my comrades and unit into the war in Iraq but the timing was such that I would have gone over the timeline and the military makes sure it no mistakes like that are made regarding soldiers slated to retire going beyond their time. To say I was sad was an understatement. My wife on the other hand, thought it was the best news

Michael and his son Marcus having fun river rafting on the
Colorado river along with other Amer-asian Christian youth.

SSG Wright's pre-retirement photo in 2003

she had heard in a long time. Thus, before I knew it, I was back in Luxembourg preparing to make our transition back to the states and out-process in Fort Stewart, Georgia. We truly were going to miss Europe, as we had forged some memorable friendships there. I had also made plans to continue my pursuit and love of flying by making preparations to attend a flight school in Fort Pierce, FL called PanAm Flight Academy. We said our goodbyes to our superiors and peers in the unit, watched our belongings loaded up and one of the NCOs shuttled us to the airport where we thanked him and boarded our plane back to the states.

It was good to be back in our home again in the US, but since we knew the movers were slated to bring our furniture and things where we designated, we had to travel to Florida to secure a new place of abode. Thus, the transition from Fort Stewart went smooth and we made our way to the flight school. The idea was to try and be as close as possible, but we were not impressed with the neighborhoods surrounding the airport where I was to train out of. So, we opted to live in Vero Beach, Florida. As of the writing of this autobiography, that is where we still currently reside.

Beloved reader, here I would like to make practical my experience, because I believe that it may be useful in helping anyone be free of the lower base addiction of lust, masturbation and their accompanying sequel of aberrant, oppressive sins. For me, it seems that when I am intrinsically connected with the Lord's work, *"the sin which doth easily beset"* me, does not. The routine always seem to be that when I become lax, hypo-vigilant and negligent in my daily devotionals, prayers and fasts, I would inevitably find myself acquiescing to those damnable temptations and afterwards, I would be extremely remorseful about my lack of strength. Happily, none of those behaviors attacked me at the beginning of our civilian life.

Sometimes I ask myself: How much damage have I done to the Lord's work with my depravations and hypocrisy and how much did I affect and hold back my wife's ministry from advancing, or mine or both?

SSG Wright, with his wife Lucy in a pre-retirement
photo, just before retiring in 2003

Sin is very damaging to the work of the Lord. Though none may know that the musician or whatever other minister may be in sin, the Lord certainly knows it, and the Devil knows it too. Just like Achan's sin caused a resounding defeat for the Israelite people, even so a lecherous man can cause great harm to the ministry of his wife or vise verse. Sometime later, I once again fell into lust. Sometimes, after my wife was asleep, (and I should have been asleep along with her). I would watch television salacious pictures or pornographic images. More recently, electronic telephones with its anonymity only served to make the situation worse. Of course, it is understood that the technological equipment in and of itself, are neither good nor bad, nor do they cause problems, but rather it is what a man or a woman does with that equipment because those items are just inanimate objects. Thus it was that I again fell again into the sin which had beset me beforehand and from my youth and it was in this condition that my wife found me anew. I foolishly thought: Now you can go to all these sites virtually without being detected and without hurting anyone's feelings or offending anyone. Those were my famous last thoughts. I forgot that we are all interconnected and that our conduct, be it good or bad, not only affects ourselves, but all of those round about us. I also forgot what the Lord himself said: "…for there is **nothing** covered that shall not be revealed; neither **hid**, that shall not be known." (Luke 12:2 KJV).

Once again, it was "by accident" that my wife surprised me watching pornography in our small office, which was hidden from the main traffic in our home. Though there were many times I had expressed with pleas my remorse and apologies and though I promised to take measures to correct this very great sin, I did not do it. This continued sporadically for years and my poor wife suffered bitterly because of my reprobate conduct. Many times I lied in order to cover this, my depravation. This time, her heart was broken terribly and I was the cause of her deep heartbreak. She had to fight with the dilemma of deciding what to do with the many, many humiliations that I caused her or; "…should I wait until he corrects himself?… The vast majority of women would have washed their hands of this matter a long time ago and that would have been the end of it. But not my Lucy. She pressed on with me all through those horrible ups and downs. She did it because she had enough faith to believe that I could rise and eventually overcome those frequent failures.

As a woman of prayer, she knew that God would give us the victory. Do you know what? She was right! I can joyfully tell you that first and foremost with the help, patience and mercy of my God, and that of my wife, and the wise counsel of a mature, seasoned pastor friend in the Lord, with time I did get the victory over this thorn in the flesh that I myself created. It was not easy. Even today, I kept a hypervigilance so as to never go back to those lascivious episodes. With my wife's agreement, these are the steps I took:

1. I ripped the computer from where it had been installed and I had it relocated in the main room of the house, where my wife could see everything and have access to verify my activities at any hour she wished to.

2. I could not be upset anytime she wanted to check on me. Otherwise, I would have been the stupid one, letting myself be crushed by this carnal corruption.

3. She would also have access to investigate my cellular android also, seeing as how it was with this item that she surprised me watching this garbage, despite the fact that at that time, she did not even know how to use it. That is why I bought her phone just like mine, taught her how to use it so that she would be up to date with all these technological advances and she could navigate mine as well.

4. We were in agreement that I should submit to disciplinary action. Therefore, I would have to abstain from taking part in any activity in the services. This was rightly so. I distanced myself temporarily from all ministerial requirements until I gained control over the situation. Though this was so, it was not so easy to do, but in the end, I overcame it with the help of God and now I can declare that I feel extremely well, knowing that these addictions were defeated.

Through all of this I understood that God was rebuking my behavior, simply by using my wife to do so. I believe that God guided us to take those steps in order to break free from those degrading vices. In truth, God was showing me how much he really loved me, because it was much more preferable that my wife reprove me and object, rather than be subjected to God's reprehension. That being said, it is good to emphasize that technology in and of itself is not bad, but the *misuse* of it, which is what gets people into trouble.

My problems were doubled by it. I would feel satisfied if this book could be of use to someone who perhaps is entangled in the damnable vice of pornography or masturbation to the end that he might know that there is a way of escape. It is not easy. Generally speaking, all those that fall into the first addiction, also fall into the second and also conjugal infidelity and possibly in sexual promiscuity. It is a slowly tightening and oppressive chain from which it is difficult to escape. In this, not only human weakness is involved, but also demonic influence. Today, as a Christian psychotherapist and minister of the Lord who was held captive by these horrible vices, I humbly advise that the following steps be considered in order to be free from pornography or any other addictive vice:

1- Recognize that you have a serious problem. So serious that it affects many in every aspect. It can cause you to lose your matrimony, your employment, your reputation and above all, your soul.

2- Confess this activity before God as a sin of lust that is capable of leading to many other sins.

3- Sincerely rush to God in prayer, asking for strength to defeat this wickedness.

4- Read the bible daily with reverence and pleas to God for wisdom in order to obey his message.

5- Vanquish without wavering all material which even hints of pornography.

6- Avoid navigating the internet's dark places, whether it be by tablet, cellular telephone or by any other means.

7- Search out a mature friend, serious, honest and loyal with whom you might talk with regarding your weakness and who will dispense advice without ridicule.

8- Learn to know the kind of spiritual warfare you're in and how to combat it using the weapons of the Spirit.

9- Occupy your time prudently to the maximum, in things which edify, And are beneficial, educative, and spiritual.

If the reader is a victim of this degrading addiction, incorporate these steps for yourself. They can help you come out of this dark ditch of pornographic addiction and its accompanying chain of degrading lust and wantonness.

As I mentioned already, we established ourselves in Vero Beach, Florida. We went in search of a permanent church home right away. After visiting quite a few, we decided to locate in a city called "Fort Pierce" FL. The name of the church's denomination was "The Pentecostal Church of God, International Mission." We remained faithful attending that congregation and after about eight month, the pastors of the church visited our home and made an offer for a pastorate in the city where we were living, that is to say, Vero Beach.

After prayer, we decided to accept the offer and we started with zero members and just went about evangelizing and talking to folks about the Lord and salvation. While working out at the gym in our apartment complex facility, I met two young ladies from Mexico and in Spanish, started talking to them about the Lord. They both were very attentive but the younger of the two was open to the idea of home fellowship. So I invited her to meet my wife and have some coffee and pastries with us. She gladly accepted it and after pouring out her heart to us, she became our first member in our church. From there it quickly grew to 8 or 9 young people. We quickly formed a little youth singing group and we won some other folks to the Lord along the way. When we reached the point of having 25 people in active communion and membership, the

Council designated us an independent church who could now sustain itself without any missionary fund assistance. That was a proud moment for us and the little church gradually grew. At times, there were people from other churches and even from our own denomination who because of various reasons, decided to join our church or become a part of our congregation. Most of these people did not help our church, but hurt it because they would always be docile in the beginning but later on, they would manifest their real reasons or motivation for being there. Some were gossip mongers, which is why they were dismissed from their previous churches. Others, thinking they were wiser than the pastorate, would try and impose their way of doing things on the congregants, which we adamantly opposed. Others still, would show up in church because of the younger pretty females and not necessarily because they loved God or wanted to worship Him. Even from the jail/prison ministry, God allowed me to make great inroads as far as seeing many prisoners saved while in the prison. These men were humble and to see and hear them speak, no one would doubt that they would fulfill every word they said regarding being faithful to God, the local church and their families once they were released.

However, upon actual release from prison or jail, it was as though they completely forgot about their commitments they had vowed. Ninety eight percent of them (according to my calculations and if my mind serves me correctly) never even so much as came by our church or any, for that matter. Many, within three weeks of being released, had a beer within their hands and were back to their old tricks. Some, sadly enough, were returned to jail and when they saw me, they hung their heads down in shame but I always told them it was God they needed to apologize to and not me, because I was nobody but a human vessel being used and a brother in the Lord fraught with human failures just like them. The two percent who did manage to call me from the countries they were deported and returned to, did remain faithful to the Lord, as far as I know, but even that only God really knows. I now understood the skepticism of other ministers who wanted nothing whatsoever to do with jail or prison ministries. They had become bitter over wasting so much time and energy over deceivers and were mad at themselves for not recognizing or discerning them for what they were. Nevertheless, the church still slowly grew and I believe the most we had in attendance was about 50. Nevertheless, it wasn't very long before someone for one reason or another did not like the way things were being done and decided to leave, most on a bad note and very few on a good note. Add to this the fact that most local churches were very liberal in their dress and moral code, and it is easy to see the difficulty in maintaining a viable congregation.

Also, at times I am sad to say, there were seeming power struggles between my wife and I, since she was officially designated as the pastor and I (because of my personal convictions and beliefs regarding the Christmas celebration, New Years and other doctrinal issues) opted to just be a brother willing to stand by her in all things. But to be honest, that position was first offered to me. I just thought it best not to cause more confusion by bringing up those issues as they were more my personal convictions than anyone else's. Mostly, whatever conflicts my wife and I had were worked out. Nevertheless, I can definitely say that there was a direct connection with my "yielding to the sin that doth easily beset me..." and anything electronic. This had nothing to do with who had the most authority in the church or any such thing. This simply was my reality of what the apostle Paul says in Romans 7:19 (KJV) "For the good that I would, I do not: but the evil which I would not, that I do.

It is difficult to describe how this works. On one side, we were trying to maintain church membership. We fellowshipped with same member churches in district and regional functions and even joined the local pastoral membership club to get to know different congregation pastors and their members. More than anything though, I believe my double minded hypocrisy was what was affecting the growth of the church above anything else. Why would God want to use a vessel given to secret carnal inclinations in his work? Would you? My wife wanted nothing more than to see a normal, healthy and happy church and so did I, but you cannot preach on Sunday about the goodness of the Lord, and on Monday, do that which is completely opposed to living holy and saintly. That leads me to share these last observances.

Conclusion

Fasting, if misused will be of no use, but if used as God prescribes it, will greatly aid in overcoming weaknesses and sin such as these I have described in this abbreviated autobiography. Even though our church membership practically went down to zero and we were placed on the missionary status, we have the faith to believe that we will once again gain lost momentum and be restored to the rightful place of prominence as a holy, God-fearing church where signs, wonders and miracles happen. We are slowly seeing church growth and relying on God's goodness and leading in this exceedingly important spiritual battle. The reader may have noticed the absence scriptural references after every sentence. I could have done that but I thought it best to display only the ones which applied to my particular situation although there are many more which could have been added to bolster this testimony. Nevertheless, I would like to leave you with one which had I applied from the beginning, I probably would not even be writing this short book. It is found in 1 Cor. 10:13 (KJV) and it states: "There hath no temptation taken you but such as is common to man; but **God is faithful**, who will not suffer you to be tempted **above** that ye are able; but will with the temptation also **make a way to escape, that ye may be able to bear it**." In closing, allow me to simply share the truths found in this powerful statement by the apostle Paul.

1   The given is that as Christians, we will be faced with temptations sooner or later (and this is already known by most Christians) but according to this declaration, if we yield to those temptations, it is not because God wills it so, but because we want to, and in my case, I ignored the way of escape that God provided me and put more attention on my own carnal lusts, to my shame.

2 It is important the we rely on the faithfulness of God, as opposed to our own supposed ability to overcome any temptations we might face, whether from within or without or sensorial.

3 It is not in God's best interest to let us suffer any temptation **more than** we can bear (tolerate, handle), because he knows the outcome to that would be that we wind up yielding to it in the long run. (*Bolden letters are mine.*)

4 Notice his love is such for us, that he has already made (planned) a way for us to escape (resist, rebuke, run away from) the temptation to the end that we can bear it. Again, had I done this, I would not be writing this sad part of my history now.

Before closing, I would like to bring to the reader's attention why perhaps within Christian circles, there may not appear to be many sympathetic ears when a brother or sister falls into sins (carnal, whatever they may be) of this nature. There is a clear and present *distinction* which should be obvious in the Christian believer's life and various passages in the bible tells us, either directly so or imply such. The following are just a few out of many more that could be cited:

Matthew 7:16 (KJV) "Ye shall know them (Who? Christians) by their fruits. Do men gather grapes of thorns, or figs of thistles? [Distinction]

2 Cor. 6:14–16 (KJV) "Be ye not unequally yoked with unbelievers: for what fellowship hath righteousness with unrighteousness? And what communion hath light with darkness? And what concord hath Christ with Belial? Or what part hath he that believeth with an infidel? And what agreement hath the temple of God with idols?… [Separation]

Ephesians 5:11 (KJV) "And have no fellowship with the unfruitful works of darkness, but rather reprove them." [Non-participation]

Obviously, as I said, many more could be added but just these few should be sufficient enough to understand that it is the holy nature of Christ in his followers which leads them to admonish or warn believers who manifest weaknesses or faults or sins such as you read about here or others not mentioned. I certainly understand their utter disdain for such ones. On the other hands, we know the great apostle Paul also expounded another great truth when he said in 1 Cor. 13:1 & 7 (KJV) that love...*beareth* all things...*endureth* all things." He also exhorted us in Gal 6:1 (KJV) "Brethren, if a man be overtaken in a fault, ye which are spiritual, ***restore such an one*** in the spirit of meekness, considering thyself, lest thou also be tempted." (*Bolden letters are mine*).

I certainly don't desire that anyone ever go through what I went through, Christian or not, nor am I looking for excuses or justification for my past conduct, but I **do** pray that within our churches they might arise ministries that deal more specifically with these types of matters, so that many who, not finding a "place of refuge", so to speak, would not be forced or obligated to seek help outside of our denomination or even in secular circles, as you read I did, not knowing where else to turn, at that time.

I pray that absolutely no one reading this book would ever be so negligent as to have similar negative experiences such as the ones described herein. It shames me to have to write about these things. James 5:16 (KJV) declares: "Confess your faults one to another and pray one for another, that ye may be healed. The effectual fervent prayer of a righteous man availeth much." I realize some may think that confession does not necessarily include a public forum where the faults are displayed but rather, privately and I agree in some instances it may not be necessary. Nevertheless, I felt led by the Holy Spirit to do so in my case, because it became part of the therapy and ultimately liberated me from my addiction, which I happily and joyfully no longer call ***mine***. I gladly gave it back to the devil, though I was a fool to have taken it in the first place. It never belonged to me, but in my weakness, I welcomed it into my life and look what damage I allowed it to do over the years and decades. Thank God you the reader are smarter than that. Presumably, no true believers

Lucy and our sons, celebrating our 25th wedding
anniversary (2008)

Lucy (seen on the extreme left) and her friends who
accompanied her to Czechoslovakia (2002)

would ever allow such mistakes to happen. Such Christians will always have my admiration; to imitate such impeccable conduct and examples are to be desired. But, if by some slime or remote chance there **is** a reader or two who falls into the minute minority of those suffering such spiritual malaise, I encourage you to embrace the escape that God has provided for us mentioned above so that you too might escape "…**the sin that doth so easily beset us**.", (whatever yours may be). (*Bold print mine*) It is still true that if we resist the devil, he will flee from us. James 4:7 (KJV) The obvious implication is that the effort to resist rests with us, seeing as how God has provided us the victory over the devil through the sacrificing of his own Son. I believe that is why later on, I gravitated towards exploring addictions and how they work. I went on to receive a Master's degree in Social Work with heavy emphasize on psychotherapy administered under different modalities in an eclectic format. Nevertheless, I always put forth biblical principles as being the **best** and **surest** way to help mental health and addictive personalities *after* becoming a Christian, I really had (nor do I presently have) no excuse to yield to temptations, given the exhortation we have in James 1:12-15 (KJV), which says: "Blessed is the man that endureth temptation: for when he is tried, he shall receive the crown of life, which the Lord hath promised to them that love him. But every man is tempted, when he is drawn away of his own lust, and enticed. Then when lust hath conceived, it bringeth forth sin: and sin, when it is finished, bringeth forth death."

These verses describe in a nutshell what I allowed to happen to me. I encourage you who may be struggling with an addiction, (whatever that may be) to walk boldly down the path of victory which God has abundantly provided us by faith in his word. Perhaps you think you've fallen so many times, you feel as though God himself has given up on you. Not so dear reader. Halleluiah! 1 John 1:9 (KJV) is still true! Have you read it lately? It says: "If we confess our sins, he is faithful and just to forgive us our sins and to **cleanse us** from **all** unrighteousness." (*Bold print mine*) I have done this even to the point of sharing it in a public forum. Some say I'm unwise for doing this for such things should be hushed up and none shall be the wiser. Perhaps for them, that might

Chaplain Michael and Reverend Lucy Wright -2016 in full ministry

be the way they would go, but I cannot not ignore the Holy Spirit's prompting that somehow, others need to hear this message. I'll gladly receive any shame that may come from this revelation, as I richly deserve it for nobody forced me to go out and do these things. One of the things that I learned from my father (may God rest his soul) that remains to me to this day is that if you make a mistake, you should always be man enough to face it and if possible, correct it. That is what I am attempting to do. If I have been bold about promoting the good things which bring glory and honor to our Lord and Savior's name, shall I shrink when it comes to the things which bring shame and dishonor, especially if I am the cause of it? I think not. So, in conclusion I once again thank you for accompanying me in this brief but heartfelt journey of testimony and confessions where I have lain bare my soul and life. My only desire in doing so is to try and help those caught in the throes of addiction and to let them know that they **can** overcome it. Why? Because Romans 8:28 (KJV) states: "And we know that all things work together for good to them that love God, to them that are the called according to his purpose." Do you love God? Of course you do or you probably would not have come this far in this book. Are you part of "those called according to his purpose?" Only you can decide that, but if you are, then even though you have "slipped and fallen" more times can you can count, even though you may feel that there is no hope because you have found yourself doing things which you know in your heart are displeasing to God, you must remember that God will **never** give up on you, as long as you don't give up on Him. Can you believe that? Do you believe that? If so, then I no longer address you as a brother or sister who has failed in the past or even one who is facing temptation on a daily basis. I address you as a conqueror; someone who though knocked down, is not knocked out and who has the internal fortitude to rise up and keep fighting and fighting until victory is obtained over the flesh, the devil and hell itself. That is who **YOU** are! Romans 8:37 (KJV) says: "Nay, in all these things we are **more than conquerors** (Bold print mine) through him that loved us." Jesus loves you, and so do I. May God richly bless you in all that you do for Him and others. If you desire to communicate with this servant,

I am available at 1 (912) 332-0271 or you can confirm friendship by searching Facebook, or contacting my email at: mcwright77@comcast.net Amen.

***Please note. Contact info is subject to change. Always use email to write us for the latest updates or text us (Lucy & I) if you have any inquires. Also, access website: keypitchtone.com for more poetry and musical information

Appendix A

The death of the beast condemned

I   Who can truly scream out loud 'gainst the monster that lies deep within? Much like the beast of the jungle who crouches, his victim unaware, is pinned. Who would sell me chains so strong that they could bind hypocrisy discreetly? Store Owner please, consider my plea, for I approach thee beseeching thy empathy.

II Many years it has been that I have heard him roar but it seems only I can perceive; and that's why he brags for he knows very well that in complaining, they'll conclude: "He' crazy!" And right they would be, for they see not the tears that at night descend like geysers; yet when sun break arises and the morning begins, none it appears, is the wiser.

III Of the harm done to self by unhealthy thoughts and my carnal and impulsive actions; and the good that a believer is supposed to display is degraded to fleshy attraction; Woe unto me! Who shall free me from the monster that only I see? Who fights me stern like the beast that he is—his death, I long it to be.

IV Thanks be to God, defeated I'm not in Christ while fasting still exists; With Jesus and his power, and the strength I derive, my inner being truly persists. I wish I could say that serving the Lord is easy, but saying so would make me a liar. But what of death? Does anyone believe its finality would be their desire?

V If you be Christian, you then are my brother and I pray that no beast you harbor; but if perchance, you are like I am, then chains you should secure through barter; and venture you must to where he dwelleth; his life, you then must end; Rejoice then we shall, with the trump at the last o'er the death of the beast condemned.

Author---Michael C. Wright/2005
Biblical Inspiration ---Rom. 7:8-25 (KJV)

Appendix B

My Heartfelt Confessions

I   My heartfelt confessions allow all those who hear, to witness my struggles with carnality; those painful concessions which opened my eyes to view the depths of pornography. It led me down paths completely devoid of prayer and spirituality; it made me ashamed, distorted my outlook and replaced reality with fantasy.

II My noted digression was ofttimes preceded by my lack of time spent searching; for the strength to resist temptation in the midst of a vice I had ended up cursing. So what was I thinking when fully aware, I allowed carnal thoughts to race? Through my mind, in my heart, up the peaks, down the valleys and then, the demons gave chase.

III My desperate obsession was hid for a while, but was destined to come to the light; for deeds done in darkness are with time exposed and brought before everyone's sight. Fool that I was, why did I descend to the depths of lust and pain? Lascivious gates that were opened by me, and I cried at the loss of my gain.

IV God's divine redirection was a flawless injection of his love I never deserved; but I reached out my hand and asked for forgiveness and to grant me his grace unreserved. My ascent from the abyss of lusts and temptations has not been a perfect affair; with relapses, trails and slippage accompanying, it was hard not to succumb to despair.

V Yet I'm now God's possession, he's heard my confessions and restored my spirituality; his divine inspiration defeats my frustrations and fills me with humility. So to all those who struggle, perhaps more than I, I implore you to ask God for help; His son Jesus will stretch his hands towards you and grant you his spiritual wealth

Michael C. Wright—Lyricist
Nov—2016
Inspiration: 1 Cor. 13 (KJV)

Appendix C

The Storms of Life

Have the storms in your life raged out of control; have the seas tossed and turned you about?

Do you fear what might happen if you don't stay your course; and you drift towards an uncharted route? Has your "ship" which was stout at the start of your journey, shown signs of damage and wear? Have you maintained the "vessel" that was given to you, or been negligent in its upkeep and care?

The thought of running aground with your "ship" is something that disturbs you inside; the rise and fall of the tempestuous waves reveal fears which you no longer hide. You remember past times when you talked with your Savior and shared with Him all your desires. Then things like ambition and goals filled your heart and your prayer life bogged down in quagmire.

You scarcely escaped the reef to your right; your ship was in imminent danger; and you know had it not been for the lighthouse of prayer, your hopes would be dashed in anger. What does it take to help you to see that the mist of the sea is misleading? Your compass is faulty, your direction misguided and the thrust that you need is depleting.

Now shame and dread have gripped your soul and you remember his name once again. You cry: "Lord, see thou not that thy son is in danger and my soul in torment and pain? Then Jesus turns and faces your storm and commands that your seas "be still." And marveled at how quickly the Savior reacts, through tears you give Him your will.

So now you go forth, you reset your course and make sure your azimuth is fine; though storms come and go and waves rise and fall, God's vision and yours' must align. The fear is gone, replaced by peace most mariners cannot ever fathom; you've avoided shipwrecking your vessel of honor, and sinking to a bottomless chasm.

M C Wright-Author/Poet/Chaplain
Biblical Inspiration---Mark 4: 35-41 (KJV)

Made in United States
Orlando, FL
25 October 2022

23834376R00066